HOME OFFICE

THE LISTENER SPEAKS:
THE RADIO AUDIENCE
AND THE FUTURE OF RADIO

Steven Barnett and David Morrison

The Broadcasting Research Unit

D1153606

LONDON : HER MAJESTY'S STATIONERY OFFICE

ISBN 0 11 340901 X

Preface

The Broadcasting Research Unit (BRU) was set up in 1980 to initiate and implement independent research into issues related to broadcasting policy. The aim of BRU is to clarify complex issues and inform the decisions of broadcasters and policy-makers.

In February 1988 BRU became an independent company limited by guarantee with charitable status. Its Board of Directors consists of representatives of a wide range of interests related to broadcasting including commercial concerns and academia as well as representatives of public service broadcasting.

BRU is funded by a combination of core grants, currently provided by the BBC, Independent Broadcasting Authority, British Film Institute and the Markle Foundation of New York, and individual project funding.

BRU has developed a tradition of large-scale empirical investigation, particularly in the field of attitudinal surveys, and cross-cultural studies.

Acknowledgements

A great many people, both within and outside the BRU, helped to produce this study. Thanks are due first to the Home Office for their willingness to fund a substantial piece of research in an area which is frequently overlooked. The result is, we hope, a significant body of original data which can serve as a base-line both for secondary analysis and for further studies in the future.

Thanks are due also to the radio executives who gave us their time and reflections on the radio industry; they have not been named individually, and I trust their identities are not too recognisable! Both the BBC and IBA were generous in providing us with a wealth of previous research and reports.

Of the many individuals who assisted us, I would like to thank in particular Anne Laking and Laura Marks for their contributions to the qualitative work; David Vick, Chairman of the Radio Academy Research Committee, for his invaluable advice and contributions throughout; Nick Moon of NOP for his tireless assistance on questionnaire design, fieldwork and analysis; Joy Mott of the Home Office for guiding us through the publishing maze; Jim McGregor of HMSO for bringing publication to fruition; and Karin Joseph for her faultless and professional proof-reading of the final manuscript.

Finally, little could have been achieved without the assistance of Alison Joseph and Cynthia Brown in supervising the production, correction and distribution of the various drafts. Particular thanks are due to them both for their efficiency, patience and good humour throughout.

Steven Barnett
Broadcasting Research Unit

December 1988

Contents

Foreword – Any Questions

The 60 year history of British radio has been characterised by a process
of gradual evolution. From a single pre-war service run by the BBC, it
has developed leisurely through the post-war addition of Light and
Third Programmes, to the four BBC streamed services which began
operation on 30th September 1967. There has been no expansion of
national UK radio services for over twenty years.

Local radio is a recent phenomenon and it, too, has undergone a
relatively gradual evolution. The first local BBC station, in Leicester,
started broadcasting in 1967 and the first local independent station, in
London, in 1973. Since then a network of commercial stations has
extended the coverage of commercial local radio to around 85% of the
population. It is not just, therefore, the concept of local radio which is
only recently established in people's minds; the concept of *commercial*
radio, financed entirely out of revenue from advertising or sponsorship,
is barely fifteen years old. There are a large number of radio listeners in
the UK who have never, whether by accident or design, heard advertisements on British radio.

In February 1987, the Government published its Green Paper en-
titled "Radio: Choices and Opportunities". This consultative docu-
ment, prompted by the imminent availability of more broadcasting
spectrum, marked the beginning of a process which will see UK radio
transformed. The plans which the Government has announced for
expanding both local and national radio represent an exponential leap in
both the number of stations and the amount of commercial air-time
which they are expected to generate. Evolution will be replaced by a
comparative revolution which will yield an abundance of choices and
opportunities.

The Green Paper raised many questions about demands and needs of
the radio audience, the adequacy of existing provision, the appeal of
more local or national services, and audience requirements for greater
range and quality of content. As part of the consultative process, the
Broadcasting Research Unit was commissioned by the Home Office to
investigate these questions. This report is the culmination of our
research.

Our study examines the role of radio in people's lives. In assessing
attitudes to and opinions about the present, it also investigates the

needs and demands of radio audiences for the future: at local and national level, amongst different sectors of the population, for every type of programme, information requirements or other roles which the radio fulfils for different audiences at different times of day. Its purpose was to allow the listener a voice in the development of new and challenging radio services which could be of benefit to every section of the community. As services expand and a new, lighter set of regulations is formulated, it is hoped that the results will be of assistance in creating the new framework for increased quantity and quality of radio services. Our sole aim was to let the listener speak.

Methodology

The project, which began in March 1987, was divided into three distinct phases:

a) Interviews with a series of senior figures within the radio industry, representing as far as possible all the constituencies of opinion within the debate. We concentrated deliberately on the Managers and Managing Directors of BBC and independent local radio stations, given their position at the sharp end of local broadcasting. As well as laying the factual groundwork for the audience research stages to follow, these interviews helped to crystallise some problems and identify others. The problems of what constituted "locality", the demands of advertisers from new services, the copyright conundrum, and the public service aspirations of many in the independent sector, all contributed to an understanding of the complexities of the debate. Chapter 11 contains a distilled analysis of these interviews. Forty were conducted in total, from the beginning of March to the end of May, and the positions and institutions of these interviewees are listed in Appendix I.

b) A short hiatus to allow for the General Election and the untypical nature of radio and television news reporting, was followed by three months of group discussions from the beginning of July to the end of September. This qualitative research method involves a moderator talking through a rehearsed list of issues with groups of 8–10 people drawn from all sectors of the population in different regions of the country. The unstructured and informal nature of these discussions, lasting about one and a quarter hours, provides a wealth of data which are both valuable in their own right and provide vital background information for the design of the subsequent questionnaire. The insights which these groups allow into listening behaviour and preferences are unique research material, and generous use is made of direct quotes from these discussions throughout the report. There were 32 discussion groups in total: a full description of where they were convened and the methodology for recruitment is contained in Appendix II.

c) The final stage consisted of a substantial forty minute questionnaire, for which National Opinion Polls (NOP) was commissioned to undertake the fieldwork. After extensive piloting in early October, the questionnaire was finalised for fieldwork at the end of October and beginning of November. The sampling was by random probability to ensure that a representative cross-section of the population was interviewed. In total, 997 respondents were successfully interviewed from an effective sample of 1542; this represented a contact rate of 65%. A full explanation of the methodology, analysis of response, fieldwork and analysis is contained in Appendix III.

In addition to the main sample, four supplementary samples were undertaken of groups who would not be sufficiently represented in the main sample but whose needs were of special interest. Thus, four small "booster" samples of people in isolated rural communities, of Asians, of Afro-Caribbeans, and of teenagers, were also interviewed. Reference to these dedicated surveys, rather than the main survey, is clearly marked in the text.

Layout of this report
Following this Foreword, the report is divided into 12 chapters. Chapter 1 examines how people use radio and the role which it plays in everyday life. Chapter 2 is an analysis of the volume of listening, how it is distributed among the different stations, and where the stations' perceived strengths and weaknesses lie. Chapter 3 is an analysis of current levels of appreciation and satisfaction with radio stations and with the service as a whole. Chapters 4 and 5 examine reactions to the prospect of particular categories of, respectively, music and speech programmes, and the effects of commercialisation on listening demand. Chapters 6 and 7 examine the whole of the local dimension in radio. Chapter 8 examines attitudes to commercial funding in radio, in particular to advertisements and sponsorship. Chapter 9 looks at the more technical problems encountered with reception, frequencies and the limits to the listener's tuning competence. Chapter 10 assesses the nature of public service commitments amongst the radio audience. Chapter 11, as stated, describes the fruits of the early interviews with industry figures. Chapter 12 contains a short summary and the main

conclusions. Finally, a short Endpiece contains some more reflective interpretations of the research which do not arise immediately from the survey data. The three appendices follow immediately after the Endpiece.

CHAPTER 1

An Everyday Story of Listening Folk

On November 14th 1922 Mr Arthur Burrows read the news, an act which would itself have constituted the major news story of the day. For the first time, live speech was being transmitted from a studio of the British Broadcasting Company, albeit to a mere handful of privileged Londoners who could afford the crystal set receiving equipment. The crackling and barely audible quality of the sound would have modern listeners scrambling for the off switch and drafting an immediate letter of complaint. At the time it was a technological miracle of stunning proportion. Even in the 1980s, anyone who has heard the measured and distant tones of Gladstone in one of the world's earliest sound recordings cannot but appreciate some of the magic which surrounded the first days of a new and fascinating medium.

The subsequent development of radio as a focus of family entertainment, as an instrument of wartime propaganda and inspiration, as a means of enabling millions of delighted followers to share the exhilaration of royal weddings and coronations, and as the basis for new and experimental forays into the world of comedy, drama, sport and news analysis, is well chronicled elsewhere. The purpose of this chapter is to examine the social context in which listening takes place in the 1980s.

Before the advent of television, radio was – amongst other things – a form of collective entertainment for the family. The historical transformation in the role of radio, displaced in its family function by television, was articulated very clearly by several older participants in the group discussions: "Things move on. I can remember a time when families used to sit round the radio in just the same way as they sit round the TV now – it's purely a change of medium, it hasn't changed the situation"; "You've got two media, one visual and one non-visual; if you want to involve yourself in the non-visual, you break up the family relationship"; "If you are going to listen to the radio you isolate yourself and that breaks down the family relationship; you then become ostracised from the family." Television has become the "social" medium, allowing the family to share a leisure activity in its own living room; radio, on the other hand, has become "asocial" – a solo medium which is isolationist rather than communal.

To describe it in such negative terms does not, however, do it justice.

1

The corollary of isolationism is comfort and company, an antidote to boredom and a solace for loneliness. In almost every group discussion, the young and old, men and women alike attested to the invaluable pleasure afforded by their radio sets in virtually every facet of their lives from first waking to late night insomnia: "If you get up miserable and that and a nice song comes on, you feel a bit happier and easier"; "I find that I'm very lethargic if I don't have the radio on with a bit of music. It gets me warmed up for my jobs. When the music is on I tend to get on better"; "I like to wake up and just be lulled into the office." Stories abounded of factories and offices where radios, sometimes surreptitiously but generally by consent, helped to alleviate an otherwise tedious and repetitive routine. Concentration was seldom a problem: "I'm doing a bit of computer programming there, and it's getting a bit boring and that, but there is Simon Bates on the radio and I'll bounce back." A postman starting work at 4.30 a.m. described the value of radio in the sorting office: "It is on for background music, for company really, because otherwise it would be a sort of dead atmosphere."

While radio at work or in the car was a tremendous boon, it was at its most valuable in the home for those (invariably women) who, in pursuit of their daytime chores, required some external stimulus and relief from solitude: "While you are doing such a menial job like ironing or potatoes or something you are lifted up a bit"; "I find I can do anything as long as the radio is on; I can clean, I can iron, I do it without noticing when the radio's on." Those women whose daily lives routinely consist of housework relied on their radios for relief from the daily domestic drudgery. As their chores take listeners around the house, the radio goes too: "I'm in all day, so if I'm doing one bedroom I've got a radio in the bedroom and then I'll move to the next bedroom and I'll put that one on in case I miss anything." For those with children, the radio provides some adult input into a world populated by children: "With having younger children I feel it is a sort of link with the outside world."

Radio, therefore, is an accompaniment to daily routine, but is also a means of mitigating feelings of loneliness. Loneliness in this sense should not be mistaken for some kind of feeling of desolation; it was no more than an uncomfortable awareness of absence of company, experienced in many different forms and degrees by many diverse people. There were housewives alone during the day; drivers whose work involves many hours in car, van or lorry; students becoming accustomed to self-disciplined study; widowed pensioners who have little everyday contact with the outside world. Animals were not exempt: "Even our dog used to like the radio when she was on her own." When radio is described in this sense, programme content is of little consequence as long as there is noise of some kind in the background –

something to alleviate the monotony of a boring job or journey, or to overcome the silence of an empty house.

People would turn to their radios in many different circumstances. The sudden and unaccustomed absence of children was a common theme: "I dreamt when they were all sort of young that one day I could just have a quiet house – but I miss the noise"; "I can't get used to dead quiet now. If everything's dead quiet I feel uneasy." These lessons are being passed down the generations. One mother was gradually helping her daughter to feel comfortable in the house on her own, despite the unnerving scraping noises of her pet hamster: "I have told her that if she's by herself and she feels it's quiet, if she keeps hearing noises, put the radio on." A teenage girl had recently moved away from home: "I'd moved into my new little room and I was lonely. I wanted someone to talk to, so I said to the radio 'talk to me'." For one teenage boy, radio could relieve simultaneously the problems of loneliness and boredom: "You've got music, keeps you a bit of company listening to people singing; otherwise it's just boring sat at home on your own doing nothing." A travelling salesman was a self-confessed addict to his car radio: "I was without one for a fortnight and nearly went off my head." For one sector of the population, for whom the world outside is somewhat more distant than most, the radio undoubtedly represents a vital source of companionship: "It was great, it was the best friend I'd ever had; I had my own cell, and the only thing I had was the radio; put it on, just listen to it and take your mind off everything." A case, perhaps, of the Home Office taking with one hand and giving back with the other.

It is important from the outset to convey the sense of intimacy which listeners have with their radios. More than one person described it, quite spontaneously, as a friend – a theme echoed by young and old alike. It was described as a reliable companion which "somehow is always there", an integral part of most people's lives: "This wireless is part of my family, it is with me"; "You feel at one with the radio but I don't think you could feel at one with the telly . . . [the DJ] is talking about certain things and you're listening, you feel that he's with you and . . . he's talking to you personally"; "It's life, it's typical. Whereas there is quite a bit of falsity about television, the radio is genuine." In this sense, to construe radio listening as just another manifestation of exposure to the "mass media" becomes inappropriate. Not only do people listen in isolation, they do it almost always as a secondary activity, a very different experience from watching television or reading a newspaper. In all its many functional guises – as entertainment, dissemination of news, relief from boredom, as immediate guide to weather and traffic conditions – it is inextricably woven into people's lives.

The concept of radio as friend, company and background noise may

3

give an erroneous impression that the nature of programme content is largely unimportant. This was true neither for speech nor for music radio programming: it was not just the medium but the programmes and presenters which formed an integral part of listeners' everyday lives. Passionate feelings were expressed about disc jockeys, phone-in hosts, quiz presenters and programme formats; at times daily patterns were constructed in order to coincide with favourite programmes. It is fair to say that not even the most casual listeners were indifferent to what they heard. The feelings of intimacy engendered by radio are attributable as much to the intimate nature of what is heard as to the flexible and private nature of the medium itself.

It was, therefore, a feature of almost every discussion group that a relatively innocuous comment would trigger discussants into spontaneous and excited expressions of opinion about familiar (and not so familiar) radio personalities and programmes. Heated and often passionate exchanges ranged from Derek Jameson's accent to Anne Nightingale's choice of records, from *The Archers* to Simon Bates' "Our Tune" (our considered opinion is that a riot would follow its once mooted exclusion from Radio 1's morning programme). The followers of these personalities and programmes would brook no criticism while their detractors would inveigh against them with equal vigour.

One man became somewhat carried away while listening in his car to a repeat of one of the old Hancock shows: "I started laughing and as I laughed there was a policeman in a car and they pulled me in – thought I was laughing at them! They took my car to pieces." A fan of Tony Blackburn explained the personal nature of his relationship with the listener: "He was going 'you out there, you' and it was just as if he was talking to you." One lady admitted that she could not wait to get back from her holiday in Spain because she missed the voices of her favourite DJs. For another the radio doctor provided a personal and intimate service superior to anything she encountered during her visits to the surgery: "He could spend a good 10–12 minutes talking to one person. To me that's better than going to the doctor for five minutes and coming out with the same tensions. . . . You feel he is talking to you personally although you haven't phoned in." A similar programme on television could not have the same effect because "you are just one of a number." And Terry Wogan could not reproduce the sense of personal interest he had acquired on Radio 2 when making the transition to television: "He has lost contact with the audience and the ordinary people; it is as though he is making up to the cameras."

While feelings ran deep about today's radio programmes, many older listeners thoroughly enjoyed the opportunity to reminisce about old favourites. Several times, nostalgic and somewhat winsome allusions were made to the family Sunday lunch accompanied by *Two-way Family Favourites*, *The Navy Lark* and *The Clitheroe Kid*. There were mournful references to the passing of *The Goon Show*, *I'm Sorry I'll Read That Again*, *Mrs Dale's Diary* and even *Music While You Work*. These outbreaks of nostalgia were not simply the traditional association of old programmes with fond memories, but a genuine commitment to programmes whose content and quality clearly imprinted themselves on the minds and memories of listeners. Modern programmes are not conceived as inferior or less entertaining than those of yesteryear; they are simply different. Reports that the BBC are planning to issue tapes of old *Dick Barton* and *ITMA* shows suggest that it has realised the commercial potential of this nostalgia.

These discussions, apart from providing excellent insight in themselves, were conclusive evidence of the attention and loyalty commanded by the programmes which people listen to. What cannot be appreciated from figures alone is the feeling of personal impoverishment that would follow from any changes which fail to take account of people's fundamental attachment to the medium.

Nevertheless, some quantitative assessment of the relative importance of radio in people's lives, and how this might vary among different demographic groups, is necessary to place the more qualitative analysis in perspective. Notwithstanding the invidious nature of any comparisons with television, as documented above, any conclusions about the role of radio would be meaningless in a vacuum. In order to establish the relative position of radio, identical questions were therefore asked about the role of television. Figure 1.1 summarises the results of these questions.

Around two-thirds of the sample believe radio is important in their lives, a little less than the equivalent response for television. The comparison also demonstrates that the *strength* of feeling is a little less widespread for radio than for television.

The most effective way of differentiating feelings for the two media is to present respondents with a simple dilemma – which would they miss

Figure 1.1
"How important do you think radio/television is in your life nowadays?"

(Base = All who have TV)

		RADIO	TELEVISION
	Base	986	986
Very important		20%	28%
Fairly important		45%	53%
Not very important		23%	24%
Not at all important		11%	4%

Figure 1.2
"If you had to give up either radio or television, which do you think you would miss most?"

Favourite Radio Station

	TOTAL	RADIO 1	RADIO 2	RADIO 3*	RADIO 4	BBC LR	ILR
Base	997	241	140	21	118	95	197
Radio	28%	22%	37%	48%	47%	24%	30%
Television	63%	66%	56%	43%	48%	65%	61%

[*Figures for Radio 3 devotees are included throughout for completeness, but the tiny subsample precludes any conclusions or interpretation]

most if required to give up one or the other? Over twice as many chose television than radio (63% compared to 28%), but the real story is contained in the responses from different subgroups. Those who would miss radio most rose to 32% in social class AB, 33% in cities, 34% in the South East and 39% in East Anglia (all variables which to some extent overlap). The most telling differences, however, are those amongst the devotees of the different radio stations; as Figure 1.2 demonstrates, Radio 2 and 4 followers are by far the most committed to radio in general. The responses among Radio 3 followers also stand out, but the tiny subsample precludes any firm conclusions: this figure should be interpreted as an approximate guide rather than a statistical truth.

The figure for Radio 4, in particular, demonstrates a commitment to radio over television which is unmatched by any other measurable subgroup. The strength of devotion to the medium amongst those with a tangible loyalty to the only predominantly speech and news station could have clear implications for future policy. If speech programming in general (as opposed to Radio 4 in particular) commands such a sense of commitment to radio, one could hypothesise that another speech station would reproduce such commitment. It is unlikely that Radio 4 has discovered the only magic formula of news, current affairs, drama etc. to satisfy listeners' appetites for speech programmes, and we shall see later how the demand for some types of speech programme remains demonstrably unsatisfied.

This figure also shows that it is not only the speech programming of Radio 4 which creates attachment to radio. Radio 2 devotees were also considerably more likely to miss radio than listeners overall, which may demonstrate a demand for more easy listening or middle-of-the-road music. For both these stations, the variance is accounted for to some extent by age differences but not completely. The extent of any such demand will be analysed later; for the moment, it is sufficient to note the major difference that loyalty to individual stations makes to listeners' attitudes to radio in general.

It must be emphasised, however, that the starkness of these figures is misleading. That most people would surrender their radios rather than their televisions should not detract from an appreciation of the integral part which the radio plays in their everyday lives. It is almost certainly its role as a secondary activity for the majority of listening time, and the corresponding use of television as a primary and vital source of leisure activity, which acounts for this relegation.

Perhaps the personal and individual nature of the medium can be best gauged by the way in which radio listeners find themselves reacting to it quite involuntarily. One by one, the listeners with whom we spoke would make the somewhat embarrassed confession that they invariably spoke to their radio. As one listener put it: "I get so involved with the radio, I ask it questions." Whether it be an anguished riposte to a totally unreasonable or contentious interviewee, the triumphant answer to an impossibly difficult quiz question or the frustrated groan at another squandered opportunity during live soccer commentary, the houses, cars, offices and factories of this country are full of people furtively locked in dialogue with their transistors.

CHAPTER 2

Analysis 1: Patterns of Radio Usage

Chapter 1 was designed to convey some of the appreciation which people feel for radio. This chapter is designed to provide the backdrop for the analysis to follow by establishing the framework of listening. The most instructive means of achieving this descriptive picture is through a graphical and statistical representation; it is vital to the understanding of the radio audience that hours and days of listening, favourite stations, reasons for listening at given times and for changing stations are understood from the outset.

A further consideration which needs to be mapped in advance is the different demographies which constitute the radio audience at any one time. We shall therefore examine how radio listening changes demonstrably amongst different age groups, social groups, ethnic groups and geographical locations as well as in accordance with different stages of the life-cycle: the processes of adolescence, marriage, children growing up and leaving home, retirement and widowhood each involve a different relationship with the world and the community which can be reflected in people's listening behaviour. It is this descriptive detail, essential for any subsequent analysis of listeners' radio needs, which forms the basis of this chapter.

The starting point for this analysis must be an examination of those people who listen to the radio at all. Overall, 4% of the sample claimed never to have heard any radio, and a further 7% to abstain from any listening nowadays. Questions on usage, preferences and enjoyment were asked only of the 89% who said they do listen to radio nowadays.

It might appear strange at first sight that anyone could honestly claim never to have listened to radio; the 11% who claim not to listen today may also appear high. The age profile of both these figures is instructive: of the 38 respondents who claimed never to have listened, 32 are aged 55 or over. The pattern is less marked for current listening, but 63 of the 108 non-listeners are again 55 or over.

The consequences of this phenomenon – that almost a quarter of retired people do not listen to radio – are possibly more important than the explanation, assuming the figure to be an accurate indicator of behaviour: it is conceivable that the more elderly respondents would be less sensitive to the question and less able to respond accurately. Other questionnaire surveys, however, have found few problems in eliciting accurate responses from retired people and it would almost certainly be as invalid as it would be patronising to ascribe these results to little more than incomprehension.

This finding is likely to be the product of three different factors. First, other research has shown that the elderly are less likely to have sets in working order; second, a greater incidence of deafness will naturally preclude radio listening for a greater proportion of this age group; and third, it is quite plausible to argue that radio was simply never part of older people's everyday experiences. A habit that was never cultivated in youth is less likely to become established in later life, especially in the absence of any social pressure to conform to the new technologies. Different arguments apply to television which is so much a primary source of leisure as well as a social lubricant that it has captivated all but the most stubborn resistors: grandparents without a television may find themselves snubbed by their grandchildren or socially isolated as conversation turns to *Coronation Street* and last night's snooker. A household without a television is an exception bordering on the peculiar; no-one asks on entering the living-room where the family radio is.

Judging by the reassuring and companionable presence which radio affords most listeners, it is ironic that the one group who could possibly derive the most pleasure are the least likely to reap its benefits. It is perhaps unfortunate that one in five 65–74 year olds and one in four of those aged 75 or over currently do not listen to radio; some benefit might accrue from drawing the attention of older people to its cheapness, its easy accessibility and the variety of suitable programming. While this may be due in part to the elderly's greater vulnerability to deafness, it is entirely possible that many elderly people associate radio with the cacophany of pop music and incomprehensible DJ colloquialisms which they sometimes find thrust upon them in High Street shops, seaside resorts or other places of social gathering. Carefully targetted information to disabuse them of such associations might be of genuine social benefit.

Turning to the 89% who do listen, Figure 2.1 shows what proportion of listeners tune in to each station as well as the proportions who have ever tried each station.

These figures are self-explanatory, but one or two are worthy of special mention. In general, just over twice as many listeners will have sampled a station as will have listened to it in the last week. This is worth bearing in mind, given the traditional emphasis by commentators on the loyalty of radio listeners to one station. It may be true, as we shall see, that listeners generally stick to one station, but many will

9

Figure 2.1
"Which of these radio stations have you ever listened to/listen to nowadays/listened to in the past seven days?"

		EVER	NOW	LAST 7 DAYS
	Base	997	997	997
BBC Radio 1		71%	37%	31%
BBC Radio 2		63%	29%	22%
BBC Radio 3		29%	8%	6%
BBC Radio 4		41%	22%	19%
BBC Local Radio		45%	22%	17%
BBC Radio Scotland/Wales		13%	5%	4%
Commercial Local Radio		55%	37%	30%
World Service		16%	3%	2%
Radio Luxembourg		42%	4%	1%
Pirate station		16%	3%	2%
Other		3%	1%	1%
None		4%	11%	16%

at some stage in the past have sampled others. Two of the figures in Figure 2.1 should be treated with caution: the 55% who have ever listened to Independent Local Radio (ILR) is artificially low, given its coverage of only 85% of the population. And the 29% who have sampled Radio 3 at some stage are not all classical music fans – many will be avid cricket listeners. It may be worth noting in passing the one in six who have tried both the World Service and a pirate station.

There are clear demographic differences, mostly a function of age and social groupings. Radio 1 emerges as unparalleled in its pervasiveness: 96% of listeners between the ages of 15 and 34 have at some stage sampled Radio 1, across all classes and regions. Whatever the criticisms of Radio 1's unadventurous playlists (and many emerged from the group discussions), it evidently strikes a chord amongst all sectors of youth. Over two-thirds of social class AB had sampled Radio 4 compared to a quarter of social class DE, and similar differentiation was apparent for Radio 3. ILR was as undifferentiated as Radio 1 but not as pervasive even allowing for its limited transmission area.

Just under two-thirds of current listeners tune in to radio every day of the week, and over three-quarters listen every weekday. Older listeners (especially the retired) are more likely to listen every day, presumably making less of a distinction between working and non-working days. Those who prefer the local stations or Radio 4 as their favourite station are also more likely to listen every day.

Radio has traditionally been recognised as a morning medium: the highest audiences are recorded in the mornings, and consequently morning advertising spots on commercial radio are the most expensive. In order to take account of the differential volume of listening during

10

different times of the day, we divided the day into morning, afternoon and evening and asked respondents for the number of minutes spent listening in each. Figure 2.2 demonstrates in graphical form how the volume of listening declines progressively throughout the day both on weekdays and during weekends.

During the week, listening declines from a peak of around one and a half hours in the morning to just over half an hour in the evenings. The same trend, starting from a lower peak, is evident for both Saturdays and Sundays. The smallest amount of listening is on Saturday evenings, averaging less than twenty minutes; while almost certainly a reflection on the attraction of television as the dominant evening medium, and the declining number of people who *want* to listen, we shall see that this is also partly due to an apparent absence of appropriate programmes.

The overall pattern of a declining audience throughout the day, and especially at weekends, is entirely consistent with listeners' perceptions of radio's role in their lives. Evenings and weekends offer the opportunity for social relaxation, in company with family and friends; while many forms of entertainment, such as film-going, watching a video, hobbies and sports involve a clearly delineated activity which satisfies the appetite for social entertainment, the isolationist nature of radio does not. This is not so much a reflection of radio's evening programming as a comment about the structure of people's lives and entertainment demands.

The downward listening trend conceals significant demographic differences, the most noticeable of which is age. Figure 2.3 shows how the daily pattern takes different forms for each age group on weekdays, Saturdays and Sundays – and demonstrates clearly how different the 15–19 year olds are. Morning listening for this agegroup is the lowest of all, an average of 70 minutes compared to 90 overall; come the evening, however, this group has the highest listening figure, with an average of 46 minutes compared to 32 minutes overall. While Saturday listening follows the overall pattern, Sunday listening is dramatically different: amongst both 15–19 and 20–24 year olds, Sunday listening actually increases to an evening peak.

For older teenagers, morning radio is less important. Perhaps, with the first experiences of independence from school and the new discipline of work, the gap between waking and departure is too short to allow for any extended listening. Perhaps also the information, news and weather functions which are such an integral part of many older listeners' morning requirements have not yet become internalised. The risk of a late train, being caught in a downpour without an umbrella or another five-mile tail-back under the Dartford Tunnel have not yet assumed the terror of disruption which interference with established

Figure 2.2

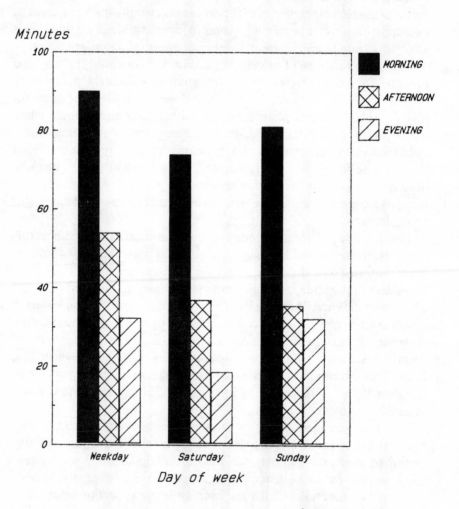

NUMBER OF MINUTES LISTENED
Each session by weekday/weekend

Figure 2.3

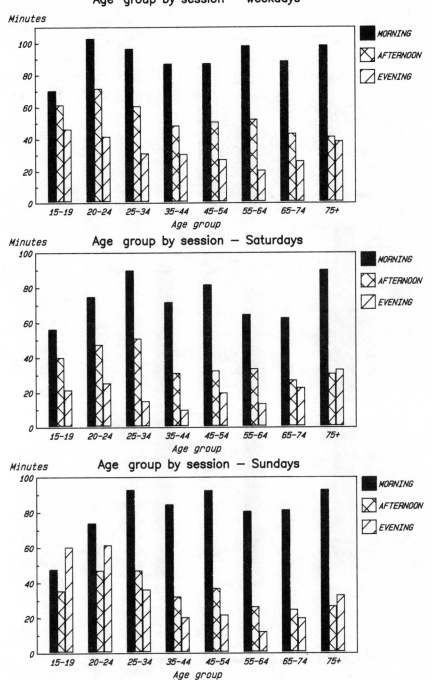

NUMBER OF MINUTES LISTENED
Age group by session — weekdays

13

Figure 2.4

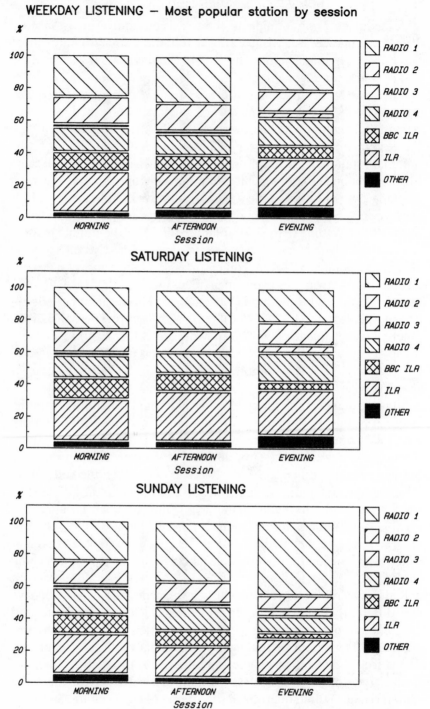

WEEKDAY LISTENING — Most popular station by session

SATURDAY LISTENING

SUNDAY LISTENING

14

routine holds for their parents. Conversely, the radio on Sunday evenings is a form of entertainment which is both cheap, accessible and superior in its programming to the television equivalent – *Songs of Praise* has not yet established a loyal following amongst the young, certainly not in opposition to the Top 40 Chart shows on both Radio 1 and network commercial radio.

Patronage of the different stations, as a proportion of total listening, changes little throughout the day. Listeners were asked, for each session of listening, which one station they listened to most often, and the results are summarised for each day in Figure 2.4. Radio 1, the dominant station in the morning, loses its position to commercial radio by the evenings – although it must be remembered that the total listening base is by this time a good deal lower. On Saturdays, ILR shows a hefty lift in the afternoon, probably a reflection of the tendency of sports fans to tune to their local station for up-to-the-minute news of the local team; the preponderance of male listeners to ILR on Saturday afternoons compared to any other time certainly supports this interpretation – twice as many men than women compared to, say, identical proportions on Sunday afternoons. This tendency is not apparent, incidentally, for BBC local radio – an example, perhaps, of the inherent disadvantage of covering a wider area which would inevitably dissipate the resources which can be focussed on individual teams. Alternatively, ILR may simply be regarded as providing a superior sports service.

Sundays demonstrate the ascendancy of Radio 1 programming in the evening. While ILR is the most popular weekday evening station, Radio 1 is preferred on Sunday evenings by nearly half of all those listening – a powerful indicator not only of the youthful nature of the Sunday evening audience, but of Radio 1's programming superiority over commercial radio at this time. Radio 4's popularity remains roughly constant throughout the day, while the quality of Sunday evening programming for the young is reflected in the disappearance of any listening to either Radio Luxembourg or pirate stations – each of which attract around 5% of available listeners on Saturday and evening weekdays.

Radio is by reputation a notoriously loyal medium. Listeners behave very differently from viewers and are generally loathe to switch around different stations, experiment, or change stations for particular programmes. The extent of this dedication changes a little, though not dramatically, depending on the time of day. As Figure 2.5 demonstrates, two-thirds of weekday morning listeners stick to the same station rising to three-quarters in the afternoon and evening. Saturday and Sunday listening is even more dedicated:

Figure 2.5
Proportion who Listen to no other Station by Time and Day

	WEEKDAY	SATURDAY	SUNDAY
Morning	65%	79%	81%
Afternoon	75%	85%	90%
Evening	79%	88%	87%

An examination of these figures on a day-by-day basis suggests that this loyalty is not quite so pronounced. During the average weekday, not much less than half of those who listen will spend at least some time tuned to more than one station; the figure declines to around a third on Saturdays and less than 30% on Sundays. Over the course of a week, more than half of all listeners will try at least one other station – and Figure 2.6 shows that the 20–54 age-groups are more prepared to switch around than the youngest or older age-groups.

Of all the stations, ILR stands out as the station which listeners are most likely to tune into as their second choice, attracting one in ten of those weekday morning listeners whose first choice lay elsewhere. No station attracts more than that for secondary listening at any time of the week, and ILR consistently comes top throughout every session.

Many illustrations emerged during the discussion groups of listeners making regular listening choices by changing stations at predetermined times of the day: "I find myself doing it automatically, just switching over like that" was one representative comment from someone who would turn from Radio 4 to Derek Jameson at the same time every day. There were similar stories about changes to Radio 4 for the *One O'clock News*, Radio 1 (from a pirate station) for *Newsbeat*, the local station for

Figure 2.6
Proportion who Listen to Different Number of Stations per Week

		TOTAL	15-19	20-24	25-34	35-44	45-54	55-64	65+
					Age				
	Base	888	106	84	152	154	118	100	165
One only		42%	42%	32%	36%	36%	36%	54%	58%
Two		39%	41%	50%	46%	42%	38%	34%	29%
Three		14%	16%	17%	13%	17%	20%	7%	10%
Four		2%	1%	1%	4%	4%	1%	2%	2%
Five		1%	—	—	1%	1%	2%	1%	1%
Six or more		*	—	—	1%	1%	—	—	—
Mean No. of stations		1.8	1.7	1.9	1.9	1.9	1.9	1.6	1.6

(* for all following tables, unless indicated otherwise, an asterisk is used to signify less than 0.5%)

phone-ins, all attesting to the ability and willingness of some listeners to discriminate.

The survey provides further evidence of the purposeful way in which people can use radio when the reasons for switching stations are analysed. 17% will change specifically for music programmes or for a different choice of music; 16% will change for a particular named programme; 15% gave the only explicitly negative response, that they wanted to avoid a particular programme or DJ or that there was nothing attractive on their first choice station. Very few (3%) are prepared simply to experiment and switch around just to see what's on, which may cause some concern as new national and local stations prepare to break the listening mould. As we explain in Chapter 8, this conservatism is founded in part on listeners' technological fears that they will be unable to return to their true home – doomed like the Flying Dutchman to travel the waves for ever. It may be a slow process to coax people out of their listening habits when so few are prepared to make unprompted forays into the unknown.

Just as identifiable groups of people use radio in different ways, so each individual's listening habits are shaped to a great extent by their own daily and weekly routines. Routines vary, and the way in which people accommodate radio into their lives varies accordingly. Figure 2.7 illustrates that the reasons given for listening to the radio will change markedly not only during the course of a day but at weekends too.

Thus, local and national news are an important part of the morning listening diet throughout the week, with declining significance as the

Figure 2.7
Reasons for Listening at Different Times of Day and Week

	WEEKDAY			SATURDAY			SUNDAY		
	Morn	Aft	Eve	Morn	Aft	Eve	Morn	Aft	Eve
Base	769	409	348	532	283	173	521	246	263
Local news	36%	21%	19%	29%	19%	16%	25%	14%	11%
National news	32%	18%	21%	25%	14%	16%	23%	13%	10%
Like prog/DJ	27%	30%	31%	28%	29%	31%	31%	38%	40%
Entertainment	24%	29%	32%	24%	27%	38%	29%	37%	38%
Background	19%	22%	14%	22%	19%	17%	19%	18%	15%
Company	18%	22%	15%	17%	16%	16%	16%	18%	12%
Pass time	9%	10%	10%	8%	8%	10%	5%	7%	8%
Traffic info	7%	4%	2%	3%	2%	1%	3%	2%	1%
Helps work	5%	9%	3%	5%	5%	1%	4%	4%	3%
Keeps alert	6%	3%	3%	5%	2%	1%	4%	2%	1%
For taping	4%	4%	7%	4%	6%	5%	4%	9%	12%
Other	5%	4%	6%	6%	12%	6%	6%	4%	5%

day progresses. The relative importance of local, compared to national news, is a finding which may be unique to radio: there are no other easily accessible sources of local news in the morning, whereas national news is available both from the morning papers and from television. At a different level, local news is a more immediate and applied knowledge which can assist people to organise their day as well as keeping them in touch with their immediate environment. This is a morning phenomenon: the fact that it declines during the day is evidence that the social enquiry element of radio news, the simple desire to 'know', is less important than the immediate practical implications; and that other means of obtaining local news – TV and newspapers – become more prevalent.

Variations in response can be explained by reference to variations in the social context of the individual. Housewives, for example, are a discrete social category whose daily existence is often bound by a limited opportunity for adult interaction. They are inhibited, too, by the geographical boundaries in which their daily work takes place. Not surprising, then, that for housewives it is the company of radio which features as the most popular reason for listening during the week: 24% gave this response for weekday mornings and 17% for weekday afternoons compared to the respective overall figures of 15% and 10%. On Saturdays and Sundays, with the benefit of family and no need for surrogate company, the proportion of housewives giving this response is no different from other groups.

For retired people, whose appreciation of the company value of radio is also higher than for other groups, these circumstances are often more permanent rather than a temporary household absence. While the roles played by housewives will vary during the course of a typical day, the world of the retired person does not involve such a multiplicity of roles. For this reason, it is not surprising that their radios constitute a source of company in the evenings as well as throughout the day.

At the opposite end of the age spectrum, young people are less concerned with the news value of radio and perceive it primarily as an entertainment medium. The rise in the total number of listeners who use radio in order to tape music on Sunday evenings is, predictably, due almost entirely to young people's reluctance to pay their respects to the copyright laws. The overall figure of 12% taping in the evenings rises to 16% amongst the 20–24 year olds and 28% amongst the 15–19 year olds.

A comparison between those whose favourite station is either ILR or BBC local radio demonstrates the major attraction of the BBC service in providing local news and information. This is not a measure of appreciation, simply a differential expression of value. While 61% of BBC local radio devotees gave local news as a reason for weekday morning listening, the equivalent figure for ILR was 49%. While the figures for both decline during the day and at weekends, the relative difference between the two remains constant.

Another index of the loyalty which listeners have for stations is the small proportion who have entirely given up listening to a station. About a third of listeners claim to have stopped listening to a station which they have once used on a regular basis. The demographic profiles of these people support the thesis that listening habits are moulded by biographical forces: the stations which stand out as most frequently left behind are Radio 1 (9%), ILR (6%) and Radio Luxembourg (13%) as well as pirate stations (6%). This stability of listening behaviour may create a substantial barrier to entry for the new players in the radio market. The good news for those who survive the initial turmoil is that the rewards for establishing an audience could be substantial: radio stations, it would appear, have to be careless indeed to lose their audiences. As on the battlefield, overrunning a position involves a good deal more resources and effort than defending it.

Desertion is generally a function of age, and explains why it is the younger pop stations which have lost their supporters. Most of these ex-listeners come from the middle age ranges 25–44, as they experience the process of transition from a relatively unencumbered existence to the more constraining responsibilities of family, work and community. The restructuring which occurs as a result of this transitional phase manifests itself, amongst other things, in changing requirements; as tastes change, so do allegiances. The more speech-based services, with an audience profile which is generally older, tend to lose listeners more rarely.

CHAPTER 3

Analysis 2: Patterns of Appreciation and the Demand for More

Radio stations, like TV channels, are traditionally assessed on the numbers of listeners. The universally accepted measure of success for a television programme is the size of audience which it attracts; quantity in radio is less of a yardstick but nevertheless is a significant factor which will influence producers and programmers of even the most minority stations. For commercial stations, whose survival depends on delivering audiences to advertisers, the size and profile of the audience is paramount.

The missing link in this assessment of success is some conception of the quality of the experience. There are many different ways of appreciating a television or radio programme which cannot be conveyed through a counting of heads, from a background buzz which accompanies more enticing activities to a total immersion more generally associated with the cinema or theatre or a gripping book. The former, while a pleasant enough accompaniment to everyday life, does not engage the emotions at any but the most superficial level. The latter can, at its most powerful, evoke feelings of elation and exhilaration which positively enhance the quality of life.

From its earliest days, television has always used some means of assessing the audience's appreciation of television programmes to supplement the cruder information emanating from the statistical department. Initially, viewers' letters were regarded as some indication of the strength of feeling and involvement with television programmes; more recently, a more sophisticated and rigorous means of measurement has been introduced, the Appreciation Index. This has been used not only as a source of information to supplement the quantitative data, but by producers and channel controllers to predict successful programmes, build audiences, and justify retention of minority programmes. Within a public service framework, as embodied by the BBC and lately by Channel 4, where audience size is not the only criterion for a decision to broadcast, the level of enjoyment and appreciation becomes especially crucial.

An equivalent indicator is less easily applicable to radio. Listeners tend not to regard programmes as discrete entities, and radio audiences are generally too small and too transient for any accurate measurement of appreciation on a programme by programme basis. The loyalty which individual radio stations command, while inhibiting any evaluation of particular programmes, does however allow for judgements of the station itself. Appreciation of a radio station is a far more appropriate, and measurable, concept than appreciation of a television channel: just as most viewers will be more attached to a television programme than its channel of origin, so most radio listeners will attach themselves more to a particular station than any of its constituent programmes.

To establish the relative appreciation and enjoyment derived from different stations, respondents in the questionnaire survey were asked how much they enjoyed those stations they listened to. The results show differential degrees of fulfilment and tend to confirm the television appreciation findings that specialist audiences will register higher appreciation scores:

Figure 3.1
"In general, how much do you enjoy listening to . . ."

(Base = All who ever listen to each station)

	R1	R2	R3	R4	BBC LR	SCOT/ WALES	ILR
Base	377	253	64	196	215	51	364
Very great deal (3)*	27%	26%	47%	36%	24%	37%	27%
A lot (2)	25%	26%	23%	30%	16%	18%	29%
Fair amount (1)	33%	33%	17%	21%	36%	33%	29%
Only a little (0)	11%	11%	8%	10%	17%	4%	11%
Don't know/No answer	4%	4%	5%	3%	7%	8%	3%
Mean	1.7	1.7	2.1	2.0	1.5	2.0	1.7

(*where appropriate, responses have been scaled and mean scores calculated in order to facilitate comparisons between subgroups)

Just under half of Radio 3's listeners register the highest appreciation response compared to just over a third for Radio 4 and the regional stations (BBC Scotland and Wales). The remainder are roughly constant at around a quarter. The overall mean, calculated in order to facilitate an easy comparison, demonstrates the greater enjoyment derived from audiences for Radios 3 and 4 compared to the other stations. The so-called minority stations, which have been pilloried for reaching a fraction of the audiences achieved by Radios 1 and 2, can take some comfort from the enjoyment they seem to provide – presumably a function of the more distinctive and more varied programming which requires greater attention and therefore a higher degree of involvement.

A less easily explicable finding is the consistently higher appreciation

21

Figure 3.2
"Is there anything about this station which you don't like? What would you change about it if you could?"

	R1	R2	R3	R4	BBC LR	SCOT/ WALES	ILR
Base	373	251	64	194	211	49	355
Nothing	54%	61%	56%	60%	57%	71%	48%

shown by women for all radio stations. Because this is not reflected to the same degree by housewives (as distinct from all women) it cannot be ascribed simply to the result of daily captivity within the home. Since the phenomenon also occurs in measurement of appreciation for television programmes, it may be no more significant than one sex being a little more generous in their capacity to praise (or a little more loathe to criticise something they enjoy).

Further evidence, not just for positive appreciation of stations but for listeners' lack of criticisms, emerges when they are given an un-prompted opportunity to rectify the faults of those stations they listen to. One might imagine that, given carte blanche to eliminate the most annoying characteristics of these stations, listeners would give full rein to a host of quibbles and complaints. It is some measure of the innate satisfaction with both the medium and the individual stations that a majority of each station's listeners could not find a single criticism.

Any particular criticism that *was* forthcoming was made by no more than a sixth of listeners to any station. The most popular complaint amongst Radio 1 listeners focussed on particular programmes or disc jockeys. The station by its nature creates relationships with listeners through the personalities of the presenters: as with any relationship, the same person can be as appealing to one individual as they are disliked by another. It was perfectly clear during the discussion groups, as almost every DJ was dissected with the knowledge and intensity of a close relation, that it would have to be a very dull presenter indeed who did not attract a few unfriendly comments. Perhaps the only surprise is that no more than 14% of Radio 1's listeners volunteered any name or programme for vilification.

Interruption of music through unwanted DJ chat was a criticism voiced by only 6% of the station's listeners, though made with some force in one or two discussion groups: "The DJs have become too big for their programmes . . . was a bigger star than the music; you felt that you should take more interest in him than what he was saying." Attitudes to the banter were somewhat dependent on attitudes to the DJ. One discussant was quite explicit about his criticisms of a female presenter: "If you tune in to her, she's more concerned about telling everyone what happened the night before, if she had her leg over or not. She's not interested in playing music, she just yaps on."

22

Restrictions on records which DJs are allowed to play were criticised by only 5%, but again emerged as a bone of knowledgeable contention during the groups. Playlists were frequently condemned, and Radio 1's lack of variety was compared unfavourably with other stations: "You used to get much better music on Luxembourg, Caroline. You used to get the records that you liked rather than the records that were decided were going to be played"; "As much as I listen to [Radio 1] now, they don't play a very wide selection of music. They have their playlist and that's it; they stick to their playlist"; "There is loads of music that you might hear in discos or clubs . . . but they don't play. Radio Luxembourg and Radio Caroline always used to play those records." One group were particularly vociferous in their criticisms of lack of variety. Young Afro-Caribbeans tended to find less to interest them on Radio 1, and found their own music tastes better served by pirate stations: "They are giving us Pick of the Pops stuff – same old stuff day after day after day. What they need is up-to-date DJs who can get the up-to-date bands . . . but at the moment a lot of the national stations are just digging up all the old records"; "It's all commercialised and like Top of the Pops . . . it doesn't cater for us."

Complaints about the DJs also featured highest for Radio 2, but again only amongst 8% of its listeners. No other complaint was made by more than 4%. The style of Radios 3 and 4 does not allow for long stints by individual presenters, and consequently complaints aimed at individuals are almost non-existent. The major criticism on both stations, albeit based on a sample of only 64 for Radio 3, is levelled inevitably at an individual programme rather than its presenter. Again, however, the numbers are very small: 9% of Radio 3 listeners and 7% of Radio 4 listeners criticised a particular programme.

No single criticism of BBC local radio was made by more than 5% of its listeners, with both individual presenters and programmes the subject of some complaint. Given the overall levels of loyalty and affection which listeners display for stations, it may be less surprising that the majority have no criticisms to make. For this reason, the proportion of ILR listeners who voluntarily complained about advertising is exceptionally high – 26% had some criticism, whether it be the quantity, the quality or the general intrusiveness. We shall describe later how this facet of commercial radio deters many from listening to it at all. For the present, it is sufficient to register the level of antagonism expressed by those who nevertheless still choose to listen.

While the different levels of appreciation were derived from *all* listeners to any one station, it might be assumed that a similar index for people's *favourite* stations would show less exaggerated differences. In fact, when listeners were asked how much they would miss their favourite radio station, the responses show very similar differences:

Figure 3.3
"How much would you miss (your favourite station) if it stopped broadcasting?"

	R1	R2	R3	R4	BBC LR	ILR
Base	242	141	22	123	95	199
A lot (+3)	49%	57%	77%	77%	59%	58%
A fair amount (+2)	29%	21%	14%	15%	20%	29%
A little (+1)	17%	16%	5%	5%	15%	9%
Not at all (0)	3%	6%	5%	3%	6%	3%
Don't know	1%	—	—	—	—	1%
Mean	2.3	2.3	2.6	2.7	2.3.	2.4

Some explanation has been offered earlier, but a further hypothesis suggests itself. The devotion and attachment demonstrated by Radio 3 and 4 listeners, while to some extent a measure of attention to programmes, may also derive from the patent lack of any equivalent type of service. A Radio 1 listener could, even if reluctantly, turn to a commercial station, or Radio 2, or their own record collection, or even a pirate station. None would be ideal, but all provide something of the Radio 1 diet. There is, however, no substitute for the in-depth news and analysis, the plays, or the information programmes on Radio 4; nor for the unique mix of talk and classical music on Radio 3. One discussant was quite explicit and echoed a sentiment expressed by other devoted followers: "If I couldn't have Radio 3, I wouldn't bother with a radio at all"; "I would write to my MP if we couldn't have Radio 3", said another who was a little taken aback at the suggestion that Beethoven might constitute a minority taste. Similar considerations apply to the regional stations: "Radio Wales is great because it's a good bit of music, a chat, the odd conversation, it's got everything." In the absence of

Figure 3.4
**"Are there any stations which you used to listen to on a
regular basis but no longer do so?"**

	Base 888
Radio 1	9%
Radio 2	4%
Radio 3	*
Radio 4	1%
BBC LR	2%
Scot/Wales	1%
ILR	6%
World Service	1%
Luxembourg	13%
Pirate	6%
None	65%

other similar options, attachment to the only existing source of pre-ferred programmes becomes more understandable.

Loyalty to individual stations, however, is not indestructible. That new commercial stations have established themselves at all in the face of both a strong national, and often local, BBC presence is an indication of some softness in commitment. Sometimes, when the opportunity is presented, the transfer of patronage has been prompted by a preference for one of two similar programming strands. Quite often, however, it appears to be age or a particular stage in the life-cycle which encourages listeners to desert one station in favour of another. Figure 3.4 shows the extent to which each station has lost some regular listeners.

The two-thirds who claim never to have given up a station is in itself surprising. The figures for the other stations reflect the process of leaving behind the youthful appetite for "pop and prattle" and graduat-ing to the less raucous, more nostalgic and generally more soothing content of non-pop stations. The graduation process is well recognised by listeners, but is obscured somewhat by the relatively recent restruc-turing of BBC national radio as well as the even more recent in-troduction of commercial radio: in twenty years time, the proportion of ILR and Radio 1 deserters could well have doubled as a new generation of ex-adolescents surrender to the nostalgia of Radio 2. A few quotes from group discussants illustrate how listeners recognise that the re-alignments taking place in their own lives are reflected in the restructur-ing of their radio preferences: "I think I'm too old for Radio 1 now"; "For years I used to listen to Radio 1 and Radio Caroline. One day you've just had enough of it and you say that's just getting on my nerves"; "I expect when the kids start getting older they'll start having it on"; "I don't like pop music, so I find that Radio 2 plays records that I can remember when I was in my teens"; "Most of the music today is for young people; they forget that the young have got to get old sometime."

Comparisons with television are as inevitable as they are invidious. While many column inches, not to mention increasing numbers of television programmes, are being devoted to an assessment of viewers' satisfaction with TV programmes, there are few equivalent evaluations of radio. Participants in the group discussions needed little encourage-ment to offer their own comparative evaluations and were consistently more critical of television content than radio content. While one expla-nation has been explored in the very different roles which the two media fulfil, another is suggested by the nature of two of the major objections to television programmes: the number of repeats and the quantity of imported product. "It's a shame that people should choose television. Obviously people must prefer watching a load of old rubbish and repeats rather than listening to something new on radio." Another

Figure 3.5
"Overall, how satisfied or dissatisfied are you with radio programmes/television programmes in general these days?"

		RADIO	TELEVISION
	Base	986	986
Very satisfied (+2)		22%	6%
Fairly satisfied (+1)		62%	54%
Fairly dissatisfied (−1)		3%	26%
Very dissatisfied (−2)		1%	11%
Don't know/no answer		12%	2%
Mean		1.2	0.2

discussant in the same group added: "They can't even fill up six hours of constructive viewing in the evening and they're talking about 24-hour TV." The young were none too happy either. One rather disgruntled seventeen year old, whose father demanded a licence fee contribution, complained: "You pay out all this fifty-eight quid for a colour licence and all you're seeing is what you've seen before. Nothing new on. Radio, it changes near enough every week – you get something new in." Another seventeen year old had weighed up the prospect of parental punishment: "I've always said to my mum – you can take the telly but don't take my radio." Radio also offered a greater range: "At any given time on television you'll have three similar types of programmes on four channels. You really don't have a choice on television, not the way you have with radio"; "I can usually find something that suits me. There is always something."

Discussants were prepared to indulge in some self-criticism of their own viewing habits, but were quick to deny that these were applicable to listening habits: "It's amazing how everyone will sit and watch some absolute garbage on television purely because it's on. Now if the radio is bad you switch it off"; "You come in", said another person, "and the thing's on and you sit around like a half moon. It's soul destroying."

The two major criticisms of television, imports and repeats, have been quantified elsewhere, and are included here as graphic examples of the unfavourable comparisons made by discussants with radio. Neither criticism is applicable to radio whose content is by nature cheaper to produce; one would therefore expect a greater level of satisfaction with radio programmes than with television, confirmed by Figure 3.5.

While different responses were predictable, the magnitude of the difference is surprising. Whether the reason be one of differential roles, cheaper programming, greater accessibility, lower expectations or some permutation of all these, that only 38 people out of 986 should

26

express *any* dissatisfaction at all is an extraordinary vote of confidence in the radio service. It is hard to imagine any other area of service to the public in which the level of disapproval is virtually non-existent.

Because dissatisfaction itself is almost imperceptible, demographic differences become difficult to measure. There is a tendency for older listeners to record greater satisfaction (33% of those over 75 were "very satisfied"), and some variations emerge from an analysis of favourite radio stations.

The differences are not great, but suggest that – for those who prefer local radio as well as Radios 2 and 4 – the programmes on offer exceed even the high levels of approval registered for radio in general. More thorough analysis of local radio needs and satisfactions will emerge from Chapters 5 and 6.

Implicit in such a high level of satisfaction is a policy dilemma which was articulated explicitly in virtually every discussion group. While the decisions about to be taken, and indeed the rationale for this research, are predicated on the sudden availability of more spectrum – and therefore the opportunity for a great deal more variety – listeners are puzzled. Since we're generally delighted with what we've got, says the Clapham omnibus man with the transistor, why give us more? The Green Paper may be concerned with choices and opportunities, but when listeners are presented with this prospect they do not enthuse. "I don't think we need any more. I think we have got a great variety" was a typical comment. One Scottish woman thought the number of local stations already exceeded requirements: "I don't see you need any more. There is Radio Clyde for the Glasgow area, and Radio Forth for Edinburgh and another one for Ayrshire which I can get as well." When the Green Paper proposals for new stations were mentioned, one group responded with unanimity: "Instead of messing about with the radio why don't they spend their time with the television. Leave it alone, don't meddle with it."

Figure 3.6
Satisfaction with Radio Programmes — by Favourite Station

	Total	R1	R2	R3	R4	BBC LR	ILR
Base	986	241	140	21	118	95	197
Very satisfied	22%	22%	27%	38%	25%	28%	28%
Fairly satisfied	62%	67%	67%	57%	72%	67%	69%
Fairly dissatisfied	3%	5%	1%	5%	2%	1%	2%
Very dissatisfied	1%	*	1%	—	—	—	—
Don't know/no answer	12%	5%	4%	—	2%	4%	1%
Mean	1.2	1.1	1.2	1.3	1.2	1.3	1.2

It must be said that the high level of existing satisfaction with content and choice does predispose some listeners to oppose any alterations to existing services. Most of the nation is not crying out for more radio. Discussants were furthermore sceptical that more stations would mean more choice, especially older listeners who drew their conclusions from their own experience of existing provision. One in particular echoed the comments of others of his generation when he noted regretfully: "I don't think there's the choice now. If you go across the dial on the radio it's nearly all music of one kind or another. I don't know how many plays there are, but I would suggest there aren't all that many." One woman opposed any new stations "if they are just going to be like Radio 1 which is a load of rubbish."

Two areas of concern are therefore perceptible in these reservations about greater choice. First, there is some scepticism that an enhanced number of stations will genuinely provide an enhanced *range* of programmes. Second, listeners are genuinely worried that any meddling with the current structure will detract from the existing services and somehow undermine an intimate part of the lives with which they feel not only contented but almost emotionally involved. This conservatism is rooted in the social dynamics of radio listening explained in Chapter 1, but is not so entrenched as to resist the introduction of new and enriching services which do not interfere with existing provision. The present and past must not only be recognisable within but imprinted upon the future.

It is always conceivable, when asking hypothetical questions about the demand for unfamiliar services, that any display of indifference is due as much to ignorance of the unknown as any real lack of enthusiasm. While wanting to obtain some quantitative measure of what appeared to be an acute lack of demand, it was imperative to include some comparative measure. The solution was to pose a question not only on reactions to the new opportunities in radio, but to similar developments in television (stretching slightly the definition of the imminent satellite channels as "three more national television channels" to ensure complete comparability). The results are the clearest possible indication that the sentiments echoed throughout the discussion groups were an accurate reflection of national feelings.

Over one in four were attracted by the prospect of more television, while less than half that figure were similarly enticed by the prospect of more national radio stations. The increasing media demands being made by the young are reflected in a significantly higher level of enthusiasm for more television – nearly half of 15–24 year olds – but only a slightly higher demand for more radio. Older viewers and listeners were less enthusiastic about both. While these figures are some

Figure 3.7
"It is proposed that there should be 3 more national television channels/3 more national radio stations/many more local radio stations. Does this ..."

	NATIONAL TV CHANNELS	NATIONAL RADIO STATIONS	LOCAL RADIO STATIONS
Base	986	986	986
Appeal a lot (+3)	28%	13%	11%
Appeal a little (+2)	26%	24%	29%
Not appeal very much (+1)	25%	28%	29%
Not appeal at all (0)	18%	31%	24%
Don't know	3%	4%	1%
Mean	1.7	1.2	1.2

indication of the direction preferred by the public for any expansion of choice, two qualifications are appropriate before the plans for expansion of radio are rendered superfluous. First, despite the very high satisfaction with current provision, over a third of the public find the prospect of more national and local radio at least a little appealing; this may be low when compared with television, but may also be interpreted as high given the levels of satisfaction. And secondly, when people are prompted in a little more detail for their reactions to categories of music or speech programmes there are signs that the appetite for radio may not be entirely satisfied. For the replete diner, the abstract concept of a more varied and larger menu is less immediately attractive than the offer of a favourite made-to-order gastronomic treat. Aural gastronomy is no exception.

CHAPTER 4

My Music: What Music Programmes do Listeners Want?

Confidence in the abundance of choice did not deter listeners in group discussions from volunteering a plethora of ideas for new programmes or stations, from hip-hop music to repeats of *Listen with Mother*. Overall levels of satisfaction conceal a latent demand for some types of music and speech programming which need to be identified. Since radio content is easily divisible into speech and music, the next two chapters look first at the demand for music radio and second for speech-based radio. This is not a simple market research approach to identifying "gaps in the market", which would not be appropriate for policy study. Policy considerations, such as the potentially dampening effect on demand of advertisements and sponsorship options, need to be assessed, as do the implications for decisions on streamed versus mixed programming.

Given the high proportion of music content on radio, it may be something of an anomaly that a quarter of listeners claim to spend less than half their radio time listening to music (Figure 4.1). Around half always or nearly always listen to music, and there is a linear progression consistent with age: the older that listeners become, the more time they spend with speech radio. The historical context of radio is relevant when looking at older people's tastes: the over 50s may well have a different perspective when they were raised on a catholic mixture of Home and Light services, supplemented latterly by the Third Programme. The development of taste is constrained by the available cultural product, which not long ago consisted of 50% speech on radio (some of it delivered, as one retired gentleman nostalgically recalled, in full evening regalia). Some of the tastes nurtured in youth can be expected to endure into adulthood, and the appetite for music radio amongst the young may represent nothing more than the speech: music ratio on radio when they were first exposed to its alluring qualities.

Again, the starkness of statistics can sometimes obscure the depth and variety of emotional attachments, and attitudes towards music on radio is a perfect illustration. A few quotes will illustrate some of the

Figure 4.1
"How much of the time you spend listening to the radio is spent listening to music programmes?"

					AGE				
	TOTAL	15-19	20-24	25-34	35-44	45-54	55-64	65-74	75+
Base	888	106	84	152	154	118	100	104	61
All (1)	17%	40%	32%	24%	15%	3%	13%	5%	5%
Nearly all (.75)	33%	34%	37%	40%	34%	39%	25%	21%	21%
More than half (.67)	11%	10%	8%	9%	13%	12%	8%	14%	15%
About half (.5)	15%	5%	12%	12%	15%	20%	25%	18%	15%
Less than half (.33)	9%	8%	6%	9%	10%	9%	8%	11%	11%
A very small amount (.25)	10%	4%	5%	5%	10%	11%	12%	19%	15%
None (0)	5%	—	—	1%	3%	5%	8%	10%	18%
Mean	0.6	0.8	0.7	0.7	0.6	0.6	0.6	0.5	0.5

appreciation and enjoyment derived from music radio, and also some of the frustration experienced by those who feel deprived of their own musical tastes.

Music programmes are appreciated by younger listeners as a means of keeping up with latest trends. One young man said he would listen to his own music selection if radio were unavailable "but I would miss the radio because that is what keeps you up-to-date with the lastest records." A young woman relies on the radio pop programmes to stave off one of the more unacceptable symptoms of ageing – not recognising a current hit: "I hate putting *Top of the Pops* on and not knowing the records – I feel old then".

Certain sections, especially of the young, make it plain that the mainstream music available on Radio 1 and ILR does not cater for their type of music or is too repetitive: "It's always been very samey, Radio 1." Radio 1 listeners were impressively knowledgeable about the existence of playlists, and were often critical not only of the restricted range of records played, but also the intervening chat – or as one teenager put it, "can't stand all that drivel between records." Accusations of narrow range were not applied universally to Radio 1 output, and certain music programmes – like John Peel's – were complimented for widening their horizons outside the popular contemporary market. The failing was often ascribed to managerial dictate rather than DJ insensitivity: "I always get the feeling that after seven o'clock they play the music they want to play rather than the playlists". Nevertheless the pirates fulfil a demand which the legitimate stations cannot – not only a diet of experimental and specialist music, but a style of presentation which is very different from the established stations. Radio Jackie and Laser, for

31

example, were described as "fresh and new" by one young man who acknowledged that the music was not particularly different. The appeal is a combination of the right sort of music mix, back-to-back records and minimum interruptions by DJs and advertisements.

At a deeper level than a demand for back-to-back music, local pirate stations seemed to fulfil a cultural need, especially amongst Afro-Caribbean communities. Undeterred by frequently poor reception and interrupted transmissions, many young (and by no means only black) listeners would stick to their pirate station: "I sometimes wonder why I listen when the reception can be so poor, but when they play good music I like them"; "Usually it's the latest music that comes on the [pirate] radio – Reggae, Soul. I don't like pop a lot"; "Some are very difficult to pick up so you don't bother. I have sometimes spent ages trying, then given up"; "If you listen to Capital, it's boring – like old time music. When you turn to pirate they have got some nice music. You can dance to it, you can do whatever you like"; "Normal radio stations just seem to go one way – it's all commercialised and doesn't cater for us."

Again, the prsentation and style is as much at issue as the content. There is a deliberate aversion to the inbred professionalism which has traditionally characterised all but the smallest of radio stations in the UK. Pirate stations "make mistakes . . . but they will talk to you in a normal voice as if I'm talking to you. Capital Radio will say, we apologise for this." This was reinforced by others: "The pirates often make mistakes and they speak to you through it"; "You can identify with them"; "When it's less professional, it makes it seem more real-istic, like you could do it yourself." For these listeners, the music derives its meaning from an identifiable culture; the station serves as a focus for distinct cultural groups who find their own tastes unreflected in the music played by existing stations. The station has an authority which legitimate stations fail to achieve, derived as much from its flexibility, spontaneity and capacity to remain fluid as from its musical content.

In addition to the cultural groups served by pirate stations, many listeners are attracted to the innate quality of specialist music *despite* the presentation: "I don't like Tony Blackburn but if you listen it's good music. Never mind about the bloke – if he is playing good music I'll listen." Content is more important than who introduces it: "On Radio London there is a bloke that plays reggae – Tony Williams – he plays good music." The fact that Williams was white came as a surprise which did not diminish the pleasure of listening.

The older generations are less dependent on music radio. While this may be the consequence of a preference for speech radio, as suggested above, there were indications that they missed the kind of programmes they used to hear and enjoy: "Certain types of music appear to have disappeared – military music has for one." A more common favourite was big band music, and one enthusiast regretted the total absence of his own passion – cinema organ music. Many older people alluded to a preponderance of pop music which they felt had displaced their own tastes: "If you turn the wireless on whatever station you get flipping pop music"; "Too much pop, it's all pop." There was even some hint that this may be one cause of the older generation's inclination to abstain from radio altogether: "I think a lot of people are put off listening to the radio because of pop music."

At the other end of the generational scale, young parents reflected on the lack of music listening opportunities for pre-teen children whose own programmes in the past were well remembered: "Tony Blackburn used to be on Sunday mornings, that was really good. *Junior Choice*. They have got rid of this now and they have got these awful teenagers and that pop panel"; "Tony Blackburn used to have younger children. And Arnold the dog, remember him?" On the same theme: "I just don't see why they can't have him back – my children would love Tony Blackburn's *Junior Choice*. You never hear The Laughing Policeman any more."

There was some feeling that the nation's children were being robbed of their childhood – that the absence of anything suitable between infancy and adolescence was depriving a generation of the gentle innocence of some delightful songs: classics like 'Tubby the Tuba', 'Sparky and the Magic Piano', 'The Runaway Train', 'Barney the Bashful Bullfrog', and 'The Old Lady Who Swallowed a Fly' have all yielded to Duran Duran and Wham. There is always the sneaking suspicion that parents would derive greater pleasure from the return of such programmes than their offspring who face stiffer competition for their affections from weekend morning television. It would be a mistake to confuse parents' interpretation of their children's tastes for their own, and Batman may well prove more irresistible to the modern child than Burl Ives and Danny Kaye.

A quantitative analysis of listeners' musical preferences does lend some credence to the argument that older people's tastes are simply not provided for. No list of musical categories can do complete justice to the range of music available, but a division into eleven discrete genres seemed to encapsulate all but the most esoteric tastes. Top of the category list for enjoyment was Pop Oldies, followed by Contemporary Chart music, Easy Listening, Classical, then Country and Western. The full list, with the proportion who claimed to enjoy each, is described in Figure 4.2 along with an approximate descriptive profile of the audience for each type of music. One word of caution is appropriate

33

Figure 4.2
"In general, which sorts of music do you most enjoy listening to?"

	POP OLDIES	CONTEMP. CHART	LIGHT & EASY	CLASS-ICAL	COUNTRY & WESTERN	CONTEMP. ROCK	BIG BAND	JAZZ/ BLUES	FOLK	OPERA	CONTEMP. SPECIALISTS
Listened to by:	43%	37%	34%	26%	22%	15%	15%	11%	10%	9%	8%
Age	25-44	15-34	45+	45+	45-75	15-34	55+	All	35-54	45+	15-34
Class	All	All	C1	AB	C2DE	All	All	AB	All	AB	C1
Favourite Station	R1/ILR	R1/ILR	R2/R4 BBC LR	R2/3/4	R2/ BBC LR	R1	R2/ BBC LR	All	All	R2/3/4	R1
Sex	Both	Both	Both	Both	Both	Both	Both	Both	Both	Both	Male

34

in analysing the potential demand for more classical music: while there may well be a considerable constituency of classical fans, there is probably an element of exaggeration in such a high figure for enjoyment. The full extent is difficult to assess, but the size indicates a greater appreciation than Radio 3 patronage might suggest.

The figures confirm older people's demand for Big Band music, established in group discussions. Country and Western was popular amongst older and heavier listeners, and especially in the C2DE social grades. Some categories appealed to all sectors of the population and might constitute the "community of interest" programming which some believe to be most appropriate for radio – Folk music and Jazz/Blues are the most obvious examples. It would be impossible in a survey of virtually any size to cover all tastes and interests: there are almost infinite variations not only of individual tastes, but of categories within categories. The foregoing can only provide an approximate guide to the boundaries of musical taste.

A measure of enjoyment will not necessarily be reflected in the demand for more of that category of music, and the following question reveals a sizeable mismatch between appreciation of different music categories and the demand for more of each category on radio. This would be an entirely predictable reflection of the current music mix: the most popular tastes are those most likely to have found a home on radio given the limited number of stations to date. Conversely, the more minority tastes are less likely to be adequately covered and may be expected to provide higher levels of frustrated demand. The expected reverse correlation, however, is not so neat, and another factor – which may simply be the strength of desire for fulfilment of a particular taste – is intruding. That is the most likely interpretation of the results summarised in Figure 4.3 which records those listeners who like each category of music according to the proportions who would like to hear more of it on radio.

According to these figures, the greatest demand is for the Big Band music most appreciated by the over 55s – even clearer evidence that the preponderance of speech radio preferred by the older generation can be ascribed as much to the absence of their ideal choice of music as to any passion for speech. The next three categories, for which there is also considerable demand, are potentially volatile fashions. The vagueness of "contemporary specialist" music could encompass a vast range of music (both hip-hop and house music were spontaneously offered in discussion groups), some ephemeral and changing almost weekly, others enduring for several years. The figures presented here constitute no more than a contemporary snapshot, and demands will inevitably change over time. Even Country and Western and Jazz, neither associ-

35

Figure 4.3

"Do you think there should be less, more, a lot more, or about the same amount of . . . currently played on the radio?"

(*Base = All who enjoy each category of music*)

	BIG BAND	CONTEMPORARY SPECIALIST	COUNTRY & WESTERN	JAZZ/ BLUES	POP OLDIES	FOLK	CONTEMPORARY ROCK	CLASSICAL	LIGHT & EASY	OPERA	CONTEMPORARY CHART
Base	128	68	200	96	388	92	132	236	88	78	333
Think there should be:											
More	41%	37%	36%	38%	30%	34%	30%	30%	24%	22%	12%
Lot more	5%	7%	9%	3%	6%	4%	3%	3%	5%	6%	2%
The same	52%	50%	53%	57%	62%	63%	64%	65%	68%	68%	80%
Less	—	3%	1%	—	1%	—	2%	1%	1%	1%	5%

ated particularly with the young, incorporate different strands of music which can be vilified and embraced with equal passion; these tastes, too, will become more or less fashionable with time and with the promotional efforts of the commercial music industry.

Perhaps these findings should be borne in mind when the allocation of radio franchises takes place; as tastes fluctuate, so will the audiences for specialist music stations, and the imposition of tight content requirements may create problems for those stations which need to retain flexibility in order to stay profitable.

When those who would like to hear more of each category of music were questioned about the appeal of a new station catering to those tastes, responses were generally similar. By this stage, the size of the subsamples, ranging from 22 for Opera to 141 for Pop Oldies, are too small to provide firm comparative conclusions. With these reservations in mind, which apply equally to Figures 4.5 and 4.6, Figure 4.4 shows that the enthusiasms for dedicated stations are fairly constant across the different musical tastes: about two-thirds of those who want more of each category would be very keen on a station which played more of it.

Attitudes to these hypothetical stations do differ, however, when the prospect of sponsorship or advertising is included in the package. Figure 4.5 illustrates how reactions to the inclusion of sponsorship might alter listeners' disposition to a station playing more of their sort of music. Resistance is higher for stations providing higher content of Light Easy music, Classical music and Contemporary Chart music, but two qualifications are imperative. First, the sample sizes are such that these conclusions can be no more than tentative guidelines rather than empirical fact. Secondly, there is no reason for assuming that this differential resistance is more contingent on the type of music rather than the sort of people who tend to prefer it. We shall see in Chapter 7 how attitudes to commercial forms of funding differ across the social groups, and these attitudes will permeate the listening base for specialist stations. Even given these caveats, the differences are large.

In general, the patterns of resistance to sponsorship are echoed in reactions to advertising, at a slightly higher level (Figure 4.6). The concept of sponsorship is difficult to convey, and the discussion groups revealed some confusion and ignorance in listeners' understanding of how it might be incorporated into radio programming. The general feeling that sponsorship would be less intrusive is reflected in the survey findings, which demonstrate a reluctance to tune in to advertising-based specialist stations from around half of those who would appreciate their content. These figures should not be interpreted as a measure of potential success or failure for such stations, only as a measure of qualification from an audience generally unaccustomed to the sound of

Figure 4.4

"If there was a new station which played more ... how much would this station appeal to you?"

	BIG BAND	CONTEM-PORARY SPECIAL	COUNTRY & WESTERN	JAZZ/BLUES	POP OLDIES	FOLK	CONTEM-PORARY ROCK	CLASSICAL	LIGHT & EASY	OPERA	CONTEM-PORARY CHART
Base	59	30	90	39	141	35	43	79	88	22	48
A very great deal	22%	33%	37%	21%	35%	20%	26%	22%	22%	41%	29%
A lot	41%	40%	29%	41%	33%	33%	42%	33%	40%	36%	38%
Fair amount	29%	17%	26%	31%	22%	37%	23%	30%	31%	18%	15%
A little	7%	3%	7%	3%	7%	3%	5%	11%	8%	—	17%
Not at all	—	—	—	—	1%	3%	—	3%	—	—	2%

Figure 4.5

"If this station was sponsored with announcements every half hour or so telling you who had helped pay for the programmes, would you be more or less likely to listen to it?"

	CONTEM-PORARY ROCK	CONTEM-PORARY SPECIALIST	COUNTRY & WESTERN	JAZZ/BLUES	BIG BAND	POP OLDIES	FOLK	LIGHT & EASY	CLASSICAL	CONTEM-PORARY CHART	OPERA
Base	43	30	90	39	59	141	35	88	79	48	22
Make no difference	60%	53%	53%	49%	49%	48%	43%	38%	37%	31%	27%
Less/lot less likely to listen	19%	30%	31%	36%	37%	36%	37%	48%	47%	54%	46%
Would not listen	—	—	4%	3%	5%	3%	—	6%	9%	2%	9%

Figure 4.6

"If this station carried advertisements, would you be more or less likely to listen to it?"

	CONTEM-PORARY ROCK	CONTEM-PORARY SPECIALIST	COUNTRY & WESTERN	JAZZ/ BLUES	BIG BAND	POP OLDIES	FOLK	LIGHT & EASY	CLASSICAL	CONTEM-PORARY CHART	OPERA
Base	43	30	90	39	59	141	35	88	79	48	22
Make no difference	42%	43%	48%	31%	37%	41%	31%	26%	27%	38%	9%
Less/lot less likely to listen	44%	40%	40%	62%	53%	48%	57%	57%	56%	56%	64%
Would not listen	2%	—	9%	5%	5%	6%	6%	13%	13%	2%	14%

commercialised radio. It would be foolish to attempt to extrapolate from these figures the behaviour of listeners of whom 2 out of 10 claim never to have heard any commercial radio.

CHAPTER 5

My Word: What Speech Programmes do Listeners Want?

Speech-based radio, by its very nature, is both infinitely varied and more difficult to categorise than music. In which category, for example, would the average listener put *Stop the Week* or *Loose Ends* or *Thought for the Day* as well as those integral parts of music programmes which consist of speech – Jimmy Young's interviews or local radio phone-ins, for instance? In addition, all programmes are subject to different interpretations by different listeners.

Whatever the appropriate categories, there was no shortage of opinions or ideas for speech programmes in group discussions. While younger listeners expressed some interest in speech generally within music programmes, most of the excited discussion emerged from the older generation. As before, the historical context of radio is important. The over 50s were raised in the "Golden Age of Radio" when the best and the brightest gravitated towards radio as the newest and most prestigious medium. Graduation from the limited audiences of the music hall, theatre or concert hall to the mass audience of national radio became a respectable ambition for any artist in the pursuit of stardom. Radio could and did create household names in comparatively little time while the music hall remained a long and tortuous journey.

Older listeners therefore enjoyed some fond reminiscences of times past, which may have influenced their preferences for speech programmes in the future. In recalling the style and quality of old programmes, and looking for some recreation of the best-loved ideas, we must beware of overestimating how many of these preferences would in reality be realised as actual listening. Cultural products are created out of and within specific settings from which they draw their meaning and their attraction. A programme which evoked immense pleasure in 1950 may seem very outdated and uninteresting in 1988 – not only by the new generations for whom such programmes have no nostalgic significance, but even for the very audiences who derived such enjoyment forty years ago. While some classics remain etched on the mind, others may seem no more than museum pieces robbed of the living force of their past.

Furthermore, the economic reality of the mass media is now transformed. Artists who forty years ago would be delighted with the oppor-

41

tunity to ply their trade on the wireless would today regard it as a secondary medium. Reputations are less likely to be established, and the financial inducements of television ensure that it attracts the most creative talent. The economic infrastructure of cultural production has been transformed, and listeners who express a (sometime passionate) desire for the types of programmes which enthralled them forty or even twenty years ago, would not necessarily listen to their modern incarnation. To ask for songs like 'The Laughing Policeman' suggests an attachment to the era of the friendly and uniformed bobby on a bicycle instead of the SPG in unmarked cars. Similarly a predilection for more comedy is likely to mean more of the old favourites (*Hancock*, *Round the Horne*, *Billy Cotton Band Show*) rather than an appetite for more Rik Mayall. When presented with the latter, some of these listeners may find their appetite for more radio comedy a little dulled. One discussant expressed the dilemma eloquently, in regretting the passing of the old solo comics: "Now Al Read, you could really laugh at his programmes. There's not very many of anything like that about; I don't think there's anyone quite as good as the older ones."

That said, and bearing in mind that these qualifications can apply to all age groups with fond memories of old radio programmes, it is instructive to convey some of the enthusiasm for the old programmes. Humour was the most powerful: "I think comedy on the radio is much greater, much better than comedy on TV. You get a programme like *Beyond the Horne* (sic), which was brilliant. I don't know whether you get programmes as good as that now." Similarly: "It's nice to have some more comedy on, you don't seem to get that now – plays and that sort of thing ... *Round the Horne* and all that." The theme was taken up enthusiastically: "That's right, and the Goons ... there's none of that sort of thing now, everything is music-based. I think that would be marvellous, there's very little of that sort of thing on the radio." One comment suggested that these programmes may have been inextricably linked with a domestic situation, rather than having any intrinsic mesmeric quality: "When I was at home the old radio always used to go on at Sunday lunchtime ... and perhaps if that sort of thing was still on I might do that as well."

Enthusiasm for speech radio was by no means rooted in the past, and there was consistent admiration for the quality and variety of modern speech radio. Many listeners confessed to the unexpected pleasure they derived from tuning in accidentally to a play or series which captivated them. Others were conscious of missing out on some very good listening through inadequate knowledge of what was on: "You think, well I've been missing all this, this is damn good this play; I'm missing some good material on this radio." Two people confessed to being late for

42

appointments as they sat in their car awaiting the imminent denouement of a play they had had no intention of listening to. Short stories had similar appeal, the possibility of finding unexpected entertainment value for short periods of time. "A good serial" also went down well, and *The Archers* aroused at least as much fervent and knowledgeable dialogue as *EastEnders* or *Dallas*.

Imagination was often mentioned as one of radio's strongest attractions, and programmes which exploited this potential were appreciated: "A play on the radio is unbeatable because of your imagination"; "Comedy on the radio is much better than comedy on television because you interpet." The point was nicely elaborated by one older Welsh listener: "Your mind creates far bigger pictures, far nicer pictures than any television camera can capture." A middle-aged London woman was listening to a murder play: "You keep looking at the door and thinking the murderer is going to come in – if that was television you wouldn't." Another young man enjoyed radio's huge potential for science fiction: "Radio is great for things like science fiction; I always loved listening to *Hitch-hiker's Guide to the Galaxy*; it was never the same when they tried to do it on telly."

This appreciation of the different potentials of the two media is extended to most categories of speech programmes, some of which are seen as highly inappropriate for the transition to television while others are much preferred to their television counterparts. Quiz shows emerged frequently in discussion groups as the ideal combination of entertainment and stimulation, even for those who despised the television incarnation; they appealed to all ages and on all stations, whether *Brain of Britain* or Radio 1's snooker quiz. Some programmes, like cookery and wildlife, were dismissed as clearly inappropriate. One young man suggested that a programme he had seen on ITV featuring someone called Roger Cook would make an excellent radio programme.

In-depth coverage of news and current affairs was generally recognised as the exclusive domain of Radio 4, and its coverage well regarded. Many felt satisfied with the existing level, but not all: "Radio 4 is mainly for current affairs and I think that there should be more." There was some evidence of greater demand for political analysis and debates later than the traditional early evening news and comment programmes: "If they were as interesting as the radio in the [early] evening I would *definitely* have that on rather than the TV." Appreciation for radio news extended beyond the depth and frequency to accuracy of both content and emphasis. Some discussants confessed to feeling more comfortable with a radio bulletin which was not dependent on the availability of dramatic pictures and could therefore order its priorities according to proper news values. "Some of your television news is slanted more, it's more sensational" was one comment, which was not an accusation of political bias but recognition of the different and sometimes distorting pressures on television news production.

Sport was perhaps the one area where, predictably, radio was forced to lag behind television. Nevertheless, the accessibility of radio sets was an invaluable asset for those wanting to follow progress in important cup-ties, Wimbledon matches, test cricket or keep in touch with racing results as they happened. Women were less enthused by this function, and one man chronicled his wife's weekly frustration with the radio: "Saturday afternoon she's whipping from station to station trying to find something other than sport."

Children's radio received support from young mothers, but is subject to the same reservations expressed about the enthusiasm for children's music. Whether or not these young women were only resurrecting their own fond memories of childhood, some were convinced that their children were losing out on a valuable source of education and enjoyment: "I think children's radio would be good ... I would like my children to be able to listen"; "There is nothing at all for children on the radio. I used to listen to *Listen with Mother*."

It must be emphasised that enthusiasm for speech programmes was not confined either to Radio 4 programmes or to older listeners. Listeners to ILR and Radio 1 in the discussion groups expressed interest in and support for topical debates or chat shows. One young London listener was keen on Sunday chat: "One of the things I really like at the moment is Capital Radio on a Sunday morning. [They have] four or five people, DJs and guests; it's just a chat show, a satirical programme if you like, but it's satire and a bit of music; it's a good couple of hours entertainment." A Radio 1 listener thought there could be more: "In the evenings on Radio 1, they have more discussions of topical issues on AIDS and things like that; there is nothing like that during the day." Other issues of current interest, such as the Poll Tax, were raised in the same vein: not a dedicated documentary or analysis programme in the Radio 4 style, but an informal approach – incorporated perhaps within a predominantly music show – which addressed issues of immediate relevance to listeners in an accessible way. Programme formats of this type were preferable because they could offer information without the effort of concentration; for some young people, this was an almost unconscious advantage of radio which enhanced their own understanding and knowledge of the world.

It is precisely this sort of nuance to listening behaviour that even the most sophisticated quantification is unable to represent accurately. The flexibility of the medium is in itself a barrier to any rigorous analysis of the infinite variety of programme formats and content preferred, and

Figure 5.1
"Which of these types of radio programmes, if any, do you ever listen to nowadays?"

	SHORT NEWS BULLETINS	PHONE-INs	SPORTS PROGRAMMES	QUIZ SHOWS	COMEDY SHOWS	NEWS IN DEPTH	DOCUMEN-TARIES	GARDENING PROGRAMMES	PLAYS	SHORT STORIES
Listened to by:	50%	28%	26%	23%	22%	21%	19%	18%	17%	16%
Age:	25+	20–54	All	All	All	25+	35+	45+	35+	35+
Class:	ABC1	C2	All	All	ABC1/2	ABC1	ABC1	All	ABC1	AB
Favourite Station:	R2/R4	BBC LR ILR	BBC LR ILR	R4/BBC LR/ILR	R2/R4	R4	R4	R4/BBC LR	R4	R4
Sex:	Both	Female	Male	Both	Male	Male	Both	Both	Female	Both

	CONSUMER PROGRAMMES	MAGAZINE PROGRAMMES	SCIENCE/ MEDICAL PROGRAMMES	ARTS PROGRAMMES	RELIGIOUS PROGRAMMES	FARMING PROGRAMMES	SOAPS/ SERIALS	PARLI-AMENT	POETRY	CHILDRENS PROGRAMMES
Listened to by:	11%	10%	10%	9%	8%	7%	7%	7%	4%	3%
Age:	35+	35+	20–74	20+	65+	55+	45+	35+	35+	25+
Class:	AB	ABC1	ABC1	ABC1/2	All	All	AB	ABC1	All	All
Favourite Station:	R4	R4	R4	R4	R4	R4	R4	R4	R4	All
Sex:	Both	Female	Both	Both	Both	Both	Both	Both	Both	Both

Figure 5.2

"Do you think there should be less, more, a lot more or about the same amount of . . . on radio?"

(Base = All who enjoy each category)

	SHORT NEWS BULLETINS	PHONE-INs	SPORTS PROGRAMMES	QUIZ SHOWS	COMEDY SHOWS	NEWS IN DEPTH	DOCUMEN-TARIES	GARDENING PROGRAMMES	PLAYS	SHORT STORIES
Base	444	248	230	205	192	188	169	164	152	140
More	12%	18%	27%	23%	31%	16%	28%	27%	34%	32%
Lot more	1%	2%	5%	2%	4%	1%	4%	4%	2%	1%
Same	81%	73%	59%	67%	58%	80%	62%	60%	61%	64%
Less	4%	4%	4%	3%	1%	—	*	2%	—	—

	CONSUMER PROGRAMMES	MAGAZINE PROGRAMMES	SCIENCE/ MEDICAL	ARTS PROGRAMMES	RELIGIOUS PROGRAMMES	FARMING PROGRAMMES	SOAPS/ SERIALS	PARLI-AMENT	POETRY	CHILDRENS PROGRAMMES
Base	96	93	90	81	68	64	62	58	37	25
More	24%	26%	29%	26%	15%	19%	13%	17%	46%	40%
Lot more	4%	—	3%	—	7%	2%	5%	—	11%	4%
Same	72%	73%	64%	68%	72%	77%	79%	76%	43%	56%
Less	—	—	*	2%	3%	—	3%	5%	—	—

the selection of quotes above represents some of the depth and richness of listeners' attitudes to speech radio which cannot be captured through questionnaire surveys. Nevertheless, despite all the qualifications about category definitions, the distorting influence of nostalgia, and the limitations of simple statistics in attempting to describe a very complex phenomenon, quantification has its advantages. By looking at the categories of speech programming which listeners claim not only to enjoy but to want more of, and by evaluating these demands in terms of age and other demographic variables, it is possible to assess the effectiveness of current radio provisions. Of even greater significance, it becomes possible to produce an approximate yardstick by which the evolution of radio in the deregulated era can be measured.

Figure 5.1 shows the popularity of each category of programme, again with a brief synopsis of the profile for each. The high proportion who listen to short news bulletins on radio may be as much a reflection of their frequency as of demand. An overall interpretation of this figure suggests that there is a greater volume of listening to the more light-hearted side of speech radio – quiz shows, comedy, short stories etc. – than to the more serious output such as science, the Arts, religious programmes or Parliament. Again, it is difficult from this figure alone to distinguish between a listening diet which reflects deliberate consumer choice and a diet which is more the product of what is available.

A far more accurate indicator of demand is the following question which asked those who listened to each category whether they wanted more or less or the same number of these types of programmes. The results, shown in Figure 5.2, demonstrate a very different pattern indeed.

The base sizes for poetry and children's programmes are too small to accept categorically that the demand is as strong as portrayed – although discussion groups did confirm, as reported earlier, a high measure of enthusiasm for the latter. More reliably, it is fair to deduce an unfulfilled demand, in particular, for plays, short stories and comedy shows as well as – to a slightly lesser extent – sport, documentaries, gardening and science programmes. By contrast, around three-quarters were content with the existing level of news programmes – both short and in-depth – of phone-ins, farming, serials and coverage of Parliament. It is unlikely to be coincidental that the programme strands most expensive to produce represent the areas of greatest need.

Once those who expressed an interest in hearing more of each category were asked their reactions to new stations including those types of programme, the base sizes for half the categories became too small for any meaningful analysis. The top ten, however, are listed in Figure 5.3 which confirms the interest in most of the categories listed above –

Figure 5.3

"If there was a new station which had more . . . how much would this appeal to you?"

(Base = All who want more of each category)

	SHORT NEWS BULLETINS	PHONE-INs	SPORTS PROGRAMMES	QUIZ SHOWS	COMEDY SHOWS	NEWS IN DEPTH	DOCUMENT-ARIES	GARDENING PROGRAMMES	PLAYS	SHORT STORIES
Base	57	50	73	51	67	32	54	51	54	47
Very great deal	19%	12%	30%	20%	15%	28%	17%	22%	30%	21%
A lot	19%	32%	34%	35%	49%	34%	33%	45%	43%	28%
Fair amount	19%	24%	19%	39%	22%	28%	39%	22%	17%	34%
Little	30%	22%	11%	4%	9%	6%	6%	10%	7%	15%
Not at all	11%	8%	4%	2%	1%	3%	–	2%	–	–

Figure 5.4

"If the station was sponsored with announcements before and after the programme telling you who had helped pay for the programme, would you be more or less likely to listen to this station?"

	SHORT NEWS BULLETINS	PHONE-INs	SPORTS PROGRAMMES	QUIZ SHOWS	COMEDY SHOWS	NEWS IN DEPTH	DOCUMEN-TARIES	GARDENING PROGRAMMES	PLAYS	SHORT STORIES
Base	57	50	73	51	67	32	54	51	54	47
No difference	46%	60%	51%	63%	52%	50%	44%	47%	46%	53%
Less/lot less likely to listen	37%	18%	33%	20%	25%	35%	34%	34%	35%	34%
Would not listen	7%	6%	3%	2%	1%	6%	2%	2%	–	–

Figure 5.5
"If there were advertisements between the programmes, would you be more or less likely to listen to this station?"

	SHORT NEWS BULLETINS	PHONE-INs	SPORTS PROGRAMMES	QUIZ SHOWS	COMEDY SHOWS	NEWS IN DEPTH	DOCUMEN-TARIES	GARDENING PROGRAMMES	PLAYS	SHORT STORIES
Base	57	50	73	51	67	32	54	51	54	47
No difference	46%	52%	55%	45%	36%	28%	31%	45%	26%	23%
Less/lot less likely to listen	39%	38%	33%	45%	55%	59%	50%	44%	63%	66%
Would not listen	7%	4%	4%	4%	1%	6%	9%	10%	2%	6%

Figure 5.6
"If there were pauses within these programmes for advertisements, would you be more or less likely to listen to this station?"

	SHORT NEWS BULLETINS	PHONE-INs	SPORTS PROGRAMMES	QUIZ SHOWS	COMEDY SHOWS	NEWS IN DEPTH	DOCUMEN-TARIES	GARDENING PROGRAMMES	PLAYS	SHORT STORIES
Base	57	50	73	51	67	32	54	51	54	47
No difference	40%	40%	44%	37%	27%	22%	24%	27%	19%	23%
Less/lot less likely to listen	44%	44%	39%	46%	59%	56%	51%	45%	61%	53%
Would not listen	9%	8%	10%	12%	6%	16%	13%	22%	13%	19%

stations with more plays, more gardening programmes, more sports and comedy shows would be very appealing to those who want more of such programmes.

The cost of additional speech programming will be borne by commercial revenue, and the nature of this commercialism for the audience is a little different than for music programming. Again, the concept of sponsorship is difficult to convey within a series of survey questions, although discussants displayed a reasonable grasp of how this might be incorporated into a speech-based service. The survey question, it must be emphasised, mentioned announcements *before and after* programmes and therefore explicitly excluded interruptions *during* a programme. Figure 5.4 shows that sponsorship on this basis will make no difference to the majority of listeners to all categories of programmes which can be analysed. Sponsored phone-ins and quiz shows would be the least vulnerable and overall around half for each category would still listen. Resistance, therefore, is more or less uniform and certainly qualified – very few claim they would not listen at all. The future for sponsored speech programmes looks optimistic.

The prospect of advertising is greeted with a good deal more reservation. For speech programmes, it was important to differentiate between commercial breaks *between* programmes (end-breaks) and commercial breaks *during* programmes. Resistance was certainly higher for the latter, but even the introduction of end-break commercials has a fairly dramatic effect for *certain* categories of speech programmes. The figures are outlined in Figure 5.5.

There are still majorities of listeners to short news programmes, phone-ins and sports programmes for whom end-break commercials would make no difference; that news figures here is not surprising since the length of bulletins would make any objections to sponsorship and advertising roughly comparable. That sports listeners feel similarly about sponsorship and advertising between programmes is a less predictable finding and might be encouraging for those advertisers for whom sports fans would constitute an important market.

By contrast, the resistance among listeners who would like more plays, short stories, documentaries and in-depth news analysis increases disproportionately so that less than a third for each category claim end-break commercials would make no difference. The pattern of objections to sponsorship is also reversed for quiz, comedy and gardening programmes. Differential effects of advertising on listeners to different categories of programme might have funding and programming implications if these levels of resistance are realised once the new series start. The demand for creative speech programmes, in particular, may be high but a reluctance to accept the only viable method of financing presents something of an obstacle which needs to be overcome.

Finally, Figure 5.6 demonstrates reactions to commercial breaks *during* programmes. The effect is comparable to attitudes to end-breaks, writ a little larger – that is, resistance rises by around ten per cent across all programme categories. Concealed within these figures is the greater *strength* of objection, reflected in the proportion who claim they would not listen to those programmes at all if they were interrupted by commercials: around one in five for plays and short stories.

The most sensible conclusion from all these extrapolations of listening behaviour in unfamiliar circumstances is that a speech-based station incorporating advertising would need to operate a cautious and sensitive policy at the initial stages so as not to offend the sensibilities of listeners unaccustomed to – and apprehensive of – the consequences of a commercially-based service. Many of the target listeners will be older and therefore unfamiliar with radio advertising; unfamiliarity breeds distrust. Once exposed to both the informational value of radio commercials and the creative quality which the best radio advertising can certainly achieve, it is not unreasonable to assume that resistance will gradually diminish. The most encouraging conclusions from these figures are the small number of listeners who would, by their own account, not allow commercial speech radio *any* opportunity to confound their worst fears.

51

CHAPTER 6

Down Your Way 1: Local Radio and the Requirements of Local Communities

Where radio becomes almost indistinguishable from patterns of daily life, rather than a medium in the same mould as television and newspapers, is the way in which it can be incorporated into local communities. We are aware of the interminable (and largely insoluble) debates that rage about the definitions of community and locality, concepts of limited analytical value to which solutions will not be canvassed here. In a study of the audience, it is the audience which frames the definitions: and in the discussion groups, participants were not limited by sociological niceties in defining the sorts of services which they expected and appreciated from their local radio stations. This and the following chapter therefore examine how listeners themselves experience local radio, the part it plays in their everyday lives, how it compares to other local institutions and media, and how listeners think they might be best served by an expanded local radio service.

Before examining audience desires and aspirations in greater detail, it is necessary to examine the social context in which local radio operates. Little is known about how comfortable people are with their chosen environments, how integrated or alienated they feel, whether the concept of being "part of the local community" even has much meaning. The parameters of people's local experience must be established as a framework for understanding not just the demand for local radio in general but also the thorny question of what form it should take.

It may come as a surprise that around 40% of people over the age of 24 were brought up in the area in which they currently live – and of the remainder who had moved to the area, a further 40% had lived there for fifteen years or more. Nearly three-quarters, therefore, have long-standing and established roots in their local area. This geographical stability is accompanied by a feeling of integration, which implies that it is not solely the consequence of economic or family constraints: over two-thirds claim to feel "completely" at home in their area, and nearly a quarter 'quite a lot'. Nine out of ten, therefore, demonstrate a positive attitude towards their local environment.

Variations for the different demographic groups are more interesting than the overall figures, and again provide a backcloth for interpretation of the subsequent analysis for these groups. The two youngest groups manifest differences which will reflect some of the variations in their listening habits. Teenagers, understandably, are much less likely to have moved into their area but feel as comfortable with it as their elders. The 20–24 age group, however, are distinctly less likely to feel comfortable, almost certainly because at this stage they are sufficiently adult to feel they have outgrown their parents' choice of environment, but have not yet developed sufficient financial independence to realise their own choices. That awkward stage of emotional independence and financial dependence has implications for listening behaviour which we return to later.

In contrast to the younger groups, the over 55s are more likely to feel comfortable with their area. It is not only age, however, which affects this sense of integration; urbanisation is also a powerful factor. Of city dwellers, for example, one in eight do not feel at home, compared to one in twenty overall. Although the difference is not quite so pronounced for large town dwellers, they too are less likely to feel comfortable. By contrast, small town and rural dwellers are more likely to feel at home in their area. Class composition, which might be expected to have an important influence, does not explain the variance as much as age or urbanisation.

These patterns, showing a tendency towards greater alienation from the community the more extensive the urbanisation, is hardly a new thesis and again will assist in interpreting local listening preferences. The concept, however, is not as self-evident as it might appear as responses to an apparently very similar question illustrate. When respondents were asked how much they *like* living in their area, the affinity implied by the previous question became somewhat muted. This time, just over half said they liked living in their area "very much", while nearly one in ten gave negative answers. Feelings of integration with an area, therefore, will not necessarily be reflected in any great affinity for it: a measure, perhaps of those who are disenchanted with their area but whose desire to move is, for economic or other reasons, frustrated.

The same demographic variations are evident on the affection question as on the comfort question: affinity increases with age and rurality. There is, however, one intriguing group of people who demonstrate how the two questions measure a subtle but vital distinction in involvement with their area. Figure 6.1 shows that those whose favourite radio station is BBC local radio are much more likely to like their area "very much" than those whose favourite station is ILR (65% v 45%).

This is certainly explicable to a large extent in terms of age, since

BBC stations have a traditionally older listening profile than ILR. For age to explain the whole difference, however, would require a similar disparity in response to the question on comfort. Although the age differential was just as marked, the equivalent responses for local station devotees was 68% for BBC and 64% for ILR. It is wiser here to note the correlations rather than hazard causal explanations. At this stage, one can conclude that either BBC local radio programmes some-how reflect or find sympathy with those who have a genuine affection for their area; or, a much less likely contention, that the nature and content of these programmes fosters a greater sense of liking for and identity with a local area. Either way, it can be safely concluded that ILR stations are generally less likely to appeal to those with a great affection for their local area.

Many group discussants were in no doubt about the importance of their local station, whether BBC or ILR, in helping to foster a sense of identity with the area. "It is directed at us", said one man, "and it makes you feel part of it." One Welsh woman said of her ILR station: "It makes you feel a bit closer to the community because they talk about the people you know and the places you know." A Birmingham man said of his BBC station: "I can picture the place as it was and certain things I didn't even know about – of course, you only get this on local radio." Another woman said she felt "much more in touch" with the station, and marvelled at the novel experience of being able to phone the station and get straight through to the DJ. Given the timing of these discussions, when the appalling conditions of the 1987 winter were only a few months past, there was universal praise for the role of local stations in bringing aid and reassurance during a miserable period – particularly vociferous in the rural reaches of Devon and Wales.

Not only extraordinary circumstances, like freak weather conditions,

Figure 6.1
"Overall how much would you say you like living in this area?"

			Favourite Station	
		TOTAL	BBC LR	ILR
	Base	997	95	199
Very much		54%	65%	45%
Quite a lot		36%	27%	45%
Not very much		7%	6%	8%
Not at all		2%	1%	2%
Don't know/no answer		1%	—	1%
Mean		2.4	2.6	2.3

Figure 6.2

"How big a part do each of the following play in helping you feel at home in this area?"

(Base = All who feel at home in this area)

	LOCAL SHOPS	LOCAL PUB	LOCAL CHURCH	LOCAL RADIO STATION	LOCAL CLUB	LOCAL COMMUNITY CENTRE	LOCAL NEWS-PAPER	FRIENDS/ NEIGH-BOURS
Play a big part	28%	11%	13%	11%	12%	4%	21%	51%
Play a part	38%	20%	21%	30%	16%	11%	48%	37%
Don't play a part	30%	65%	63%	53%	62%	71%	30%	12%
Don't know/isn't one	4%	4%	2%	5%	8%	13%	1%	*

Figure 6.3
Importance of Local Radio in Helping People Feel at Home – by Class and Locality

	TOTAL	CLASS				LOCALITY				
		AB	C1	C2	DE	CITY	SUBURB	LARGE TOWN	SMALL TOWN	RURAL
Base	942	188	223	238	291	105	236	111	169	319
Local radio station										
Plays a bit part (2)	11%	7%	8%	14%	15%	17%	14%	7%	10%	10%
Plays a part (1)	30%	27%	30%	31%	32%	32%	28%	33%	30%	31%
Doesn't play a part (0)	53%	63%	57%	50%	45%	50%	53%	53%	51%	55%
Don't know/isn't one	5%	1%	1%	1%	2%	—	5%	7%	9%	4%
Mean	0.6	0.4	0.5	0.6	0.7	0.7	0.6	0.5	0.5	0.5

but everyday problems were considered the ideal material for local radio, in stark distinction to the limited usefulness of national radio. One discussant said: "It felt part of the community, Radio Tees. I used to like tuning in just to see what was going on – things like *I'd better stay away from town*, general local matters", and added ironically, "It's OK Radio 1 presenting something about a sixteen-mile tail back on the M4 or M1." Approachability was another important factor, again in contrast to national radio: "You sometimes see the presenters walking about and you can identify with them, talk to them. They are more approachable whereas [with] Radio 1 you never see the guy, he is just a voice. The only time he goes round anywhere is when he's getting £500 to open a boutique." Another discussant made the comparison with newspapers: "It's the same difference between reading the *Birmingham Mail* and reading the *Daily Mail*: the *Birmingham Mail* is more interesting as far as I'm concerned because that's an area I know."

These ringing votes of confidence, expressed in discussions explicitly devoted to radio, need to be placed in a wider context to be fully understood. There are many factors which assist in helping people to identify with their area, and the local radio station is only part of a complex interrelationship. In an effort to assess the *relative* significance of local radio against a catalogue of other local influences, the questionnaire survey suggested a list of local institutions and asked respondents to evaluate the importance of each in helping them to feel at home in their area. At this stage of the interview, there was no indication that radio was to constitute the main focus of the questions. Figure 6.2 shows how the local radio station comes some way behind friends/ neighbours and local shops (not surprisingly), but more significantly well behind local newspapers.

Despite the enthusiasm expressed in discussions, therefore, the importance of local radio must be kept in proportion. Even allowing for the overstatement of religious fervour, the fact that the local church plays a big part for slightly more people than the local radio station in helping them to feel comfortable is some measure of its limited effect.

Again, the generality of these statistics obscures some significant variations among subgroups. There are two groups of people for whom local radio is more likely to constitute an important factor – the lower social grades, and city dwellers. Figure 6.3 shows that 17% of the latter and 15% of the former claim local radio plays a big part in helping them to feel comfortable with their area.

While still constituting a small proportion of these groups, this is still comparatively greater than the total. Causal hypotheses should again be resisted, but the correlation itself is important: those who are most likely to feel out of touch with their local area are also more likely to claim that local radio helps them stay in touch. An indication, perhaps, of the potential role of local stations in the metropolitan areas.

Figures from the three minority group samples suggest that, while some neighbourhood factors have a different impact from that registered in the main sample, the role of local radio is very similar. Amongst the Asian community, 13% said that local radio played a big part in helping them feel at home, and 38% that it played a part. Greater weight was given to the local temple and local shops, both perhaps reflecting the major focus of cultural identity for Asian communities. Results from the Afro-Caribbean survey showed a slightly greater impact for the local church and local community centre. The rural group reinforced the traditional stereotype by placing the local pub higher than the main sample, and to a lesser extent the local church.

The role that local stations might play in helping to integrate listeners into the community is one that has implications for many areas of social life, and differences between the two types of local station could assist in understanding which elements of local radio can most effectively contribute. Too much significance should not, at this stage, be placed upon the figures in Figure 6.4 which shows that BBC local radio devotees are more likely to claim that local radio contributes to their feeling of

Figure 6.4
Importance of Local Radio in Helping People Feel at Home – by Favourite Local Station

	Favourite Station	
	BBC LR	ILR
Base	93	187
Plays a big part	31%	22%
Plays a part	53%	48%
Doesn't play a part	16%	27%
Don't know/isn't one	—	4%

Figure 6.5
"I am going to read out some different types of information which people use. For each one can you say how important this type of information is to you in your daily life?"

		WEATHER FORECAST	WHAT'S ON TV	WHAT'S ON RADIO	PROBLEMS ON PUBLIC TRANSPORT	ROAD+ TRAFFIC CONDITIONS	JOB VACANCIES	WHAT'S ON CINEMA/ THEATRES	LOCAL EVENTS
	Base	997	997	997	997	997	997	997	997
Very important (3)		25%	21%	10%	17%	27%	12%	6%	9%
Fairly important (2)		41%	46%	30%	22%	34%	14%	24%	33%
Not very important (1)		9%	6%	17%	25%	13%	47%	35%	23%
Not at all important (0)		9%	6%	17%	25%	13%	47%	35%	23%
Don't know/no answer		*	*	*	*	1%	1%	*	*
Mean		1.8	1.8	1.3	1.3	1.8	1.0	1.0	1.3

58

integration than ILR devotees. As we shall see, this is likely to be more a function of the type of station and type of listener it serves than any measure of the intrinsic merit of the station.

An integral part of the local radio system as currently established in the UK is its role in servicing the day-to-day requirements of the local community. There was a catalogue of local news and information needs which was reiterated by almost every discussion group: weather reports, traffic reports, announcements of local events, the progress of local soccer or cricket teams, an efficient means of selling that unwanted fridge or picking up a bargain. The importance of up-to-date knowledge about the worst traffic jams and the current state of the local motorway contra-flows rarely went unmentioned in discussions, and Figure 6.5 confirms this as the most important type of local information.

Road and traffic conditions came top of the list, closely followed (in the best of British traditions) by the weather and TV guide. Regional and demographic variations followed predictable patterns: road conditions were of less interest to the 15–24 years old and weather information was especially important to rural dwellers and older people. Information about public transport, though of less importance overall, was demonstrably more important to suburban dwellers, the 15–24 age group and those in DE social grades. Information on job vacancies was of little relevance to most people over 24, a function both of the non-specialist types of jobs advertised and the extent of youth unemployment.

Different minorities have different information requirements, supported by evidence from the special supplementary surveys. Information about job vacancies was more important for Asians and much more so for Afro-Caribbeans – 28% and 40% respectively said this was very important information compared to 12% nationally. Black respondents also seemed to regard information about radio programmes as more important. The more isolated residents in the special rural survey confirmed the conclusions drawn from rural respondents in the main survey: great concern about information on the weather in their area and local events.

While local radio's flexibility and immediacy were regarded as tremendous advantages in group discussions, other sources emerged which in many cases rendered some of the information almost superfluous. As they did for many years before the introduction of the wireless, other sources can provide a perfectly adequate focus for keeping in touch with the local community: "We have a parish magazine which comes out once a month, that gives you all the information. Posters go round. We have about five post boards around the village, there are two

Figure 6.6

"Which of these do you mainly use to get information about . . ."

(Base = Those for whom each type of information was very/fairly important)

	WEATHER FORECAST	WHAT'S ON TV	WHAT'S ON RADIO	PROBLEMS ON PUBLIC TRANSPORT	ROAD + TRAFFIC CONDITIONS	JOB VACANCIES	WHAT'S ON CINEMA/ THEATRES	LOCAL EVENTS
Base	660	669	394	394	608	261	303	411
TV	67%	14%	—	7%	19%	2%	3%	2%
National Radio	13%	2%	13%	5%	17%	*	—	*
Local Radio:	24%	2%	17%	28%	47%	6%	4%	11%
BBC	(12%)	(1%)	(7%)	(10%)	(22%)	(2%)	(1%)	(4%)
ILR	(12%)	(1%)	(10%)	(18%)	(25%)	(4%)	(3%)	(7%)
National Paper	5%	49%	32%	2%	1%	9%	7%	1%
Local Paper:	5%	27%	19%	26%	9%	91%	93%	85%
Bought	(5%)	(22%)	(17%)	(16%)	(7%)	(61%)	(60%)	(50%)
Free	*	(5%)	(2%)	(10%)	(2%)	(30%)	(33%)	(35%)
Radio/TV Times	—	14%	14%	*	*	—	*	—
Teletext	7%	7%	3%	1%	4%	*	2%	—

shops you can advertise in." Again: "You hear all the news when you go to the shop or the church." Local newspapers include, of course, freesheets: "I don't think listening to the radio would make much difference. I read the local paper which is even more local than the radio station."

Anecdotal evidence of the relative importance of local radio is of less value than a more reliable quantitative assessment. When respondents in the questionnaire survey were asked about the main sources they used for those areas of information which were important to them, local radio featured for three types of information: weather, transport and traffic problems (Figure 6.6).

This should not be interpreted as a restricted role for local radio in catering for the information requirements of the population. It is significant that local radio is by far the most popular source for the most useful information (road and traffic problems), and is on a par with the local paper for information on transport.

What the figures again cannot convey, but which is implicit in any comparison between the relative effectiveness of radio and newspapers in delivering information, is the recognition among group discussants that radio can keep up with and broadcast problems of immediate relevance and urgency. One woman's son went to an Adult Training School on a special bus: "Nine times out of ten . . . they'll break off and let you know whether the buses are running. It's important to me to know what's going on." One Glasgow inhabitant relied on information about the state of the roads, given his confirmed opinion that roads are "either damaged or dug up. . . . It's a pastime in Glasgow digging up streets." A Swansea man changed his listening behaviour according to the season: "In the winter I listen to Swansea Sound for the weather reports and that sort of thing. . . . I put on Swansea Sound twenty minutes before I am due to leave." In the summer, when there is no risk of disruption from the weather, the radio stays off. There were explicit comparisons with the shortcomings of the local papers for those whose time was better spent elsewhere: "The information that you can get on the radio is instant, you haven't got to stop and look and listen." And: "I don't have the time to physically sit down and read the paper to get information from it." In short, whatever the advantages of the local paper, it cannot predict four-mile traffic queues on the M1 or the cancellation of the 16.32 into town. Furthermore, although the figures relegate local radio to second place as a source for weather information and local events, the reinforcing nature of announcements made on local radio is perceived as a valuable service to the local community.

Information requirements are not the same as news requirements, and most people like to be kept abreast of local as well as national and

61

Figure 6.7
"How important is it for you to know about these different types of news?"

	WORLD NEWS	NATIONAL NEWS	LOCAL NEWS	SPORT NEWS	FINANCIAL NEWS
Base	997	997	997	997	997
Very important (3)	37%	45%	37%	17%	10%
Fairly important (2)	43%	44%	50%	21%	26%
Not very important (1)	17%	9%	11%	31%	35%
Not at all important (0)	3%	2%	2%	30%	29%
Mean	2.2	2.3	2.2	1.3	1.2

international events. This was clear from the group discussions and is confirmed by Figure 6.7, with some interesting variations in response to the different types of news.

Most people claim to be interested in the general news areas, but interest is highest for national news. The British reputation for insularity is not assisted by the relative position of world news behind both national *and* local news, although there is evidence to suggest that news priorities are comparable in other countries. For present purposes the greatest significance lies in the absolute level of interest in local news: over a third of respondents claim that local news is *very* important to them, and a further half that it is fairly important.

When analysed demographically, local news emerged as especially important for one group in particular: over half of those whose favourite station is BBC local radio said that local news was very important to them, compared to 37% overall. This cannot be a function of the different age profile of BBC local station listeners, since the age analysis shows no equivalent strength of feeling amongst older people. The equivalent figure for ILR is 42% – considerably lower than the BBC, but again higher than average. Local radio, on this evidence, does indeed play a crucial part in fulfilling the local news demands of listeners, but to different degrees. The differences between BBC and ILR are examined in more detail below.

Both the rural survey and the results among Afro-Caribbeans show a greater demand for local news amongst these groups – 47% and 45% saying it was very important compared to 37% nationally. This was not at the expense of an interest in national and, especially, international news and suggests perhaps a greater sense of dependence on and constraint within their local neighbourhood.

Just as the local paper is of major importance for local information, similarly for local news. Figure 6.8, which examines the main sources of information for the different news categories, is conclusive on two issues: both national and local radio are only subsidiary sources of

Figure 6.8
"Which of these (sources) do you mainly use to get . . ."

(Base = Those for whom each type of news was very/fairly important)

	WORLD NEWS	NATIONAL NEWS	LOCAL NEWS	SPORTS NEWS	FINANCIAL NEWS
Base	800	888	874	383	355
TV	82%	78%	29%	60%	43%
National Radio	13%	12%	2%	7%	8%
Local Radio:	4%	5%	21%	11%	4%
BBC	(2%)	(3%)	(12%)	(7%)	(2%)
ILR	(2%)	(2%)	(9%)	(4%)	(2%)
National Paper	26%	28%	3%	33%	46%
Local Paper:	1%	3%	58%	18%	6%
Bought	(1%)	(3%)	(36%)	(14%)	(5%)
Free	(*)	(*)	(22%)	(4%)	(1%)
Teletext	2%	2%	*	4%	8%

information for national and international news after television and newspapers. Secondly, and less predictably, local radio is used by less people than local papers *and* television as a source of *local* news. It is a reflection both of the power of television and, perhaps, of the still underdeveloped awareness of local radio that local television coverage (covering by definition a much larger area than local radio) still provides the more popular source of local information.

It is also possible that for many people, a concern for local news extends beyond the locality served by their local stations – that the wider transmission area and news coverage of the commercial TV station is better able to fulfil their own definition of 'local' information requirements. The next chapter, which examines attitudes to local news and information, suggests that many people wish to escape what they see as the constraining parochialism of their immediate environment and have wider boundaries for their personal definitions of locality. For such people, the television (supplemented perhaps by the local paper) may be quite local enough.

Figure 6.9
Sources used for Local News by Favourite Local Station

	BBC LR	ILR
Base	91	181
TV	26%	26%
BBC LR	46%	6%
ILR	5%	27%
Local Bought Paper	26%	35%
Local Free Paper	14%	17%

Reference was made earlier to differences between ILR and BBC local radio. A comparison of local news sources for the devotees of each suggests that the local station is of considerably greater use and importance for BBC listeners than for those of ILR as a source for local news.

For BBC local radio devotees, their favourite station is by far the most popular source of local news. For ILR devotees, their station is less often used than the local paper and on a par with television. These differences reflect the earlier findings that BBC local radio fans are more likely to like their area, and all these differences demand some consideration.

Age is, undoubtedly, a factor. In our view, however, it would be a mistake to reduce the patterns emerging from this data to a function of age; a crucial factor is the life-cycle of individuals which induces a feeling for and immersion in the local community. As individuals attain financial independence, exercise their own life choices and begin to put down roots in a given area, as they become more reliant on local transport, employment and services, and more involved in their area, then their radio demands will change accordingly. The local radio station provides the information necessary for conduct of daily life as well as a source of information for social activities. The requisite level of news and information services does not come cheap, and the parlous state (at least until recently) of ILR financing perhaps inhibits the most effective coverage. Furthermore, the older profile of an audience established within the local community will be of less intrinsic value to advertisers – the consumption patterns of the over 55s, for example, compare unfavourably with 25–45s.

The suggestion is not that the information needs of younger people are less, simply that they are different and may therefore be more easily satisfied elsewhere. It was clear from discussions that local radio *was* a valuable provider of information on, for example, local clubs, job vacancies and youth advisory services. It was more important, however, as a means of entertainment which appeals to and is located in a specific age group – not just as "pleasurable listening" but as a symbolic expression of identity. Through music young people relate to others in their age group and through types of music to types of individuals within their age group.

Given this preference for music-based entertainment, the information requirements take second place. Local music stations without any information focus may provide younger listeners with a quandary: while we have already established the demand for more of different strands of music, a specialist station without any roots in the local community would deprive some youngsters of a valuable source of information and advice.

For older people, radio is located less as a means of identity in their age group and more as a means of identity with the neighbourhood in which they have a higher material stake. The evidence adduced above seems to show conclusively that a speech-based local station, providing the sort of local news, information, help and advice services which might assist the more established local citizens in the administration of their everyday lives, is essential. It is difficult to say whether one such station is sufficient to satisfy the desire for local news and information, but the costs may well preclude any more.

The foregoing analysis is subject to one very significant proviso: whatever generalisations are made about where people derive information and news of the local area, the differences seem to be substantial in different regions of the country. Regional variances should generally be treated with some suspicion, especially given the subsample sizes of those for whom local news is important. Nevertheless the size of the discrepancies cannot be ascribed solely to differential sample sizes, and Figure 6.10 demonstrates some vastly differing regional habits for keeping in touch with the local area.

The only consistent lesson from this figure is that local radio nowhere matches the popularity of TV or newspapers. From the complete dominance of local papers in Scotland to the prevalence of TV in the North and freesheets in the South East, the regional characteristics are patently different. It is in this unpredictable environment that the new local stations will have to operate.

In order to understand properly the nature of this competition, comparison of local radio with the local press is of greater relevance than comparison with television. In audience terms, of course, this is not strictly true since at certain times of day television and radio compete directly for audience attention. Over the last five years or so, with the advent of breakfast and daytime television, radio in general has faced an encroachment from television in the very hours in which it was traditionally strongest.

In revenue terms, however, local radio does compete with the local press. Although the ratio of national:local revenue varies between stations, the vast majority of the smaller ones rely for at least 50% of their income on local or 'retail' advertising. The rates charged by newspapers serve as a benchmark for local advertisers, and constrain the charges which radio stations can make. A common complaint from stations in the North, who insisted that their sales teams attracted a greater quantity of advertising, was the inadequate revenue which such enterprise produced because of the low rates the station was forced to charge in order to remain competitive.

While there may be no direct competition between local radio and

Figure 6.10
Sources used for Local News – by Region

	TOTAL	SCOT-LAND	NORTH	YORKS +HUMB	EAST MIDS	EAST ANGLIA	SOUTH EAST	SOUTH WEST	WEST MIDS	NORTH WEST	WALES
Base	874	85	55	80	42	50	221	87	102	107	45
TV	29%	9%	58%	29%	21%	38%	24%	37%	31%	21%	42%
BBC LR	12%	6%	13%	8%	21%	16%	14%	16%	8%	11%	7%
ILR	9%	8%	11%	10%	2%	8%	7%	7%	16%	14%	7%
Local Bought Paper	36%	65%	25%	45%	38%	28%	30%	38%	33%	32%	36%
Local Free Paper	22%	4%	2%	14%	17%	30%	40%	11%	27%	29%	2%

local press for audiences, their respective roles within the community are interesting. For the local audience, there is a clear distinction not only between local radio and local press, but also between paid-for newspapers and freesheets. Figure 6.11 shows the relative importance of each type of local radio and each type of newspaper.

There is more commitment to the local bought paper than any of the other local media. Given the financial transaction required, and given the very different editorial styles which the two types of local paper represent, it may be expected that similar commitment would not be displayed for freesheets. In asking how much each of the local media would be missed, we obtain an indication of their relative value to the local community. On this basis, bought papers emerge as more highly valued than either BBC or independent local radio, which in turn are placed higher than freesheets. The attraction of freesheets, which would be missed by nearly half of those who read them, is intriguing given their unannounced imposition on householders: they do not apparently go the way of appeals from American Express, double glazing companies or the other numerous purveyors of junk mail.

The paucity of formal news, as opposed to listings and information, might render freesheets redundant for many newspaper readers. Their relative popularity suggests, however, that the information they provide may not represent "hard news" but is of value. In extrapolating this evidence to a narrower definition of local news and information, one might reasonably conclude that local stations without traditional newsrooms and news values, but still providing a forum for the circulation of local information, may be equally valuable. Such stations could not, it must be emphasised, supplant current levels and detail of news content which the figures above imply *are* appreciated by the local community; they could, however, operate within a different framework

Figure 6.11
How much Respondents would miss Local Stations v Local Papers

(Base = All who ever listen to each station/read each paper)

		Local Stations		Local Papers	
		BBC	ILR	Bought	Free
	Base	307	430	713	739
A lot		29%	33%	42%	22%
A fair amount		19%	23%	26%	23%
A little		30%	24%	19%	26%
Not at all		22%	19%	12%	27%
Don't know		★	★	★	2%

Figure 6.12
How much local bought paper would be missed – by Age and Class

		TOTAL		AGE						CLASS			
	Base	713	15-24	25-34	35-44	45-54	55-64	65+	AB	C1	C2	DE
A lot		42%	29%	39%	39%	49%	39%	60%	34%	40%	42%	51%
A fair amount		26%	31%	25%	29%	21%	29%	21%	29%	28%	24%	24%
A little		19%	25%	23%	19%	17%	13%	12%	22%	19%	20%	14%
Not at all		12%	13%	10%	13%	10%	18%	8%	13%	12%	14%	10%
Don't know		2%	3%	4%	1%	2%	—	—	1%	2%	1%	1%
Mean		2.0	1.8	2.0	2.0	2.1	1.9	2.3	1.9	2.0	1.9	2.2

of news, and attract a different kind of audience. There are implications in this analysis for the ecology of radio broadcasting which may well be materially disturbed if existing stations with a commitment to more thorough and traditional news coverage are forced to cut back. This is discussed in more detail in Chapter 11.

The demography of those who are most likely to miss local bought papers (Figure 6.12) suggests that the more economically and physically restricted – social classes DE, the retired and housewives – occupy a world whose boundaries are more tightly drawn and therefore may have a comparatively greater interest in their immediate surroundings. For these people the local paper represents the means of communication with that part of the world perceived to be of most relevance to them. Exactly the same patterns of response emerge from the demographic analysis of those who would miss local freesheets.

The foregoing analysis has been applied to the different demographic groups where relevant, but two groups of people in particular require more detailed and extensive analysis: radio listeners in London, and members of discrete ethnic groups, in particular Asian and Afro-Caribbean groups. Because a survey of this size cannot hope to reflect the huge diversity of populations within the capital, analysis of the former must rely on the discussion groups. Analysis of the latter is derived both from discussion groups and the special surveys; for the quantitative data, as ever, the size of the sample and traditional difficulties in recruitment of small groups should counsel caution in interpretation.

Londoners in general expressed a good deal less sympathy for any concept of community or neighbourhood feeling. The city itself was considered too wide and sprawling, covering a massive diversity of classes and cultures and tastes, for any radio station (or for that matter TV station) to recognise or reflect a unity of common geographical purpose and need. Perceptions of two stations, Capital and LBC, were more akin to perceptions of Radio 1 and Radio 4 than any of the

68

comparable radio stations in other areas: a music station and a news station, rather than two recognisably London stations. BBC Radio London was not widely listened to, and a few were even surprised by its existence. One suburban Londoner was explicit: "I don't think there's much community feeling. Capital, although it's a local radio station, doesn't feel like a local radio station. It's not at all really." Another inner London resident did not think a London-wide station could make anyone feel part of the city: "It's too big a place to be able to feel part of – you only feel part of the district you actually live in." A woman in the outer London suburbs expressed a similar sentiment a little more brutally: "My friends ... down past Maidstone all listen to the local radio; I feel it's more for people who are the country bumpkins."

Any meaning attached to the concept of community was very limited, confined to the immediate row of houses, high-rise block of flats or even to a particular corridor within a block. Even the concept of a district community, as for instance within Wandsworth, was not received with any enthusiasm, although it is fair to say that few discussants could think of any particularly enticing programme material that the Borough of Wandsworth might offer. The problem with the Capital seems to be two-fold: mobility between districts is greater, so that there is no great loyalty for or identity with a particular suburb or district. And the sheer size of the population and geographical area means that there cannot be one focus of local attention: whereas most large towns or even cities will boast no more than two football teams, one cricket team, one or two general hospitals, a town hall, one or two professional theatres and a long list of other civic, sporting and cultural institutions, London has an abundance. A sporting example will illustrate the difference. While London is unlikely to celebrate an Arsenal victory in the FA Cup (an eventuality likely to create more grief than joy, given the number of followers of rival London teams), the city of Coventry was united by their team's arrival in the final of last year's competition. This community of spirit can be reflected by the radio, and one man who rarely listened to ILR described how he tuned to Mercia for commentary because it could identify with and reflect the buzz which infected the whole city.

Finally, London's fulcrum position as the national political and financial centre, as well as inhibiting the potential development of any sense of "belonging", has parallel repercussions in the rest of the country. A few complaints were registered in different regions about the London-centred nature of national news, and how distant and detached these reports were from the "real" problems and concerns of the local people. One Radio Leeds listener, for example, said: "National radio is I think very based down South." Thus, one persuasive reason

69

for listening to local radio was by definition absent for Londoners. The somewhat tentative conclusion, requiring further investigation, is that London needs somehow to be served on a slightly different basis from other areas, perhaps in a way that reflects the diversity not only of geography but of cultures. The existence of ethnic cultures is not, however, confined to London and constitutes the second area to which special attention should be paid.

On the evidence available both from the discussion groups and the surveys of Asian and Afro-Caribbean minorities, there is a substantial demand for ethnic radio – that is, radio dedicated to the specific requirements of ethnic cultures. We should acknowledge from the outset the limitations of this research whose scale could not possibly encompass the many different and diverse cultures in the British popu-lation. There are sizeable communities, to name but a few, of Greek and Turkish Cypriots, of Chinese, Jewish and Irish people all of whom have claims to special treatment. Their exclusion from this research is not a reflection of any lack of demand, simply of lack of resources to under-take an exhaustive examination of every ethnic group. The analysis which follows may well be extendable to any or all of these groups, but will require further research for validation.

There are a number of pirate radio stations which already attest to the unsatisfied demand for certain types of ethnic music and entertain-ment, in particular of Afro-Caribbean style. There do seem to be black communities which rely heavily on these stations not only for entertain-ment but also for information of local ethnic events. The survey results given below confirm the emphasis which many black people place on local and pirate radio. Some ILR and BBC stations, in particular in metropolitan areas with significant ethnic populations, attempt to pro-vide some ethnic programming which is generally not regarded as an adequate substitute among the Afro-Caribbean population.

As with the young in general, music is especially symbolic for this group. Reggae is preferred and appreciated not just in some musicologi-cal sense but as a point of self identity. Pirate stations were appreciated as much for the style of presentation, very different from mainstream pop broadcasting, as for the musical content. One black Londoner listened regularly to a pirate station and saw it as a model: "It would make me feel more at home, like Sky. The guy is obviously black, the way he talks makes me feel at ease. He is not formal but more like 'I'm here to play music, I hope you like it'. He is down to earth." The amateurish style, the admission of mistakes, the breaks in transmission to avoid the authorities were all part of the fun, although having to relocate the new frequency could be a bore. It is important to emphasise that illegality itself was not part of the intrinsic enjoyment, although it

70

cannot in truth be said to have interfered; it was the spontaneity and most of all the values espoused which gave these stations their allure: "When it's less professional it makes it seem more realistic, like you could do it yourself."

The popularity of the pirate stations is emphasised by the survey of Afro-Caribbeans: 45% said that they listened to pirate stations "nowadays", and 14% were prevented from listening to one or more pirate stations because of bad reception (since there is likely to be some overlap between these two figures, they cannot be aggregated to give an overall picture of demand). Such special provision that is made by radio and television is appreciated: 75% say they watch TV programmes aimed especially at black people, and 56% listen to specially directed radio programmes. Music radio is more important than speech-based: just over a quarter said that all the radio they listened to was music-based.

Amongst the Asian community, there is a different emphasis on the type of service preferred. Ethnic music would certainly be enjoyed, even by the younger generation brought up in the UK on Madonna and Wham: "There are new sounds coming in, new Indian music; I know my friends would like that a lot." Music would, ideally, be only one strand of a service which should contain a variety of ethnic content. There was a good deal of enthusiasm for more detailed news reporting from India and Pakistan not currently satisfied by the necessarily Anglocentric press and broadcasting services of this country. One man described the pleasure his grandparents used to derive from an Asian Sunday morning TV programme: "That was their pride and joy, just to listen to the half hour of BBC1 . . . where they could learn and understand something that meant something to them, a little bit of back home." Similar feelings were expressed about sporting contests and achievements. There was support for stories, plays, cookery programmes, information about new Indian films, religious programmes and programmes in Hindu and Urdu.

In other words, a strong cultural content would be welcome which would, it seems, be applicable to and appreciated by all age groups. If done well it could attract non-Asian listeners and help to bridge a comprehension gap between cultures; a programme on arranged marriages, for example, could have great education value, "helping non-Asians to learn about our way of life." We were struck by the strength of support for such a station not just from the older members of the community – some of whom found difficulty in understanding English and had spent much of their youth in Asia – but from the younger, totally assimilated Asians who followed their parents' and grandparents' cultural traditions with some interest. In the survey of Asians,

71

16% claimed to have difficulty in understanding spoken English; this group, in particular, are thereby disenfranchised and must take refuge in the pictures of television for their news and information. One man described his mother who had lived here for 22 years: "She would never understand [radio]. She watches the English *News at Ten* even though she doesn't understand it; at least she can see the pictures. If she is interested in something she will ask you to translate."

The survey confirms all the group discussion findings. Asian language programmes on the radio found favour among 58% of Asians, but this demand is not founded simply on a poor understanding of English. When asked about English language programmes, 56% wanted such programmes on radio – as illustrated above, a means of helping non-Asians to understand Asian culture as well as providing a valuable service to the English-speaking Asian community.

A problem recognised by the Asians themselves is that the diffuse nature of their communities would render many of them out of reach of any local or community Asian station. Although still wedded to many of their own customs and traditions, some Asian families are moving out of the urban areas and integrating with the more traditional indigenous culture. A further problem of a similar nature will inevitably provide irreconcilable difficulties for the new Radio Authority. Some small Asian communities, for example in a town the size of Southampton, will almost certainly be competing for frequencies against rival contenders with equal claim to serve a different local community with other types of music or speech-based programming. By what criteria will the referee decide? If the decisive factor is numbers, the smaller ethnic communities will lose out. If it is profitability, those commanding the greatest economic strength and of most relevance to local advertisers could win the franchise at the expense of larger but poorer communities. The research highlights a difficult regulatory dilemma, but may also be exploited to suggest a structural compromise using one of the available national networks. Such a proposal should not be construed as a direct consequence of this research, and is therefore contained in a supplementary Endpiece at the end of the report.

CHAPTER 7

Down Your Way 2: Pleasures and Prospects of Local Radio

It is always difficult to convey to respondents, both in discussion groups and particularly in surveys, a concept or set of circumstances which is outside their immediate comprehension. The prospect of more radio, we have seen, did not set listeners alight with anticipation, and this is no less likely to apply to local as to national radio. Within certain limits, however, imaginations can be fertile; and it was, of course, perfectly acceptable to inquire into the criticisms and complaints currently associated with local radio.

However listeners may conceive a very local station, very few were captivated by the prospect. Time after time in discussion groups, participants would register their apathy and sometimes outright hostility to the concept of very local stations focussed on the immediate locality. "But there is nothing ever happening down here" was a common response echoed in many areas around the country. Given the logical response from a participant in the same group, "There might be but we just don't know about it", a teenage girl was in no doubt about the limited usefulness of the information which would be forthcoming: "All you would get is what jumble sale is on up the road at the Church and what Hawaiian night was on at the Rose and Crown." Those who lived in the tight communities of rural Devon or Staffordshire, for example, were the most dismissive: 'You don't want to be very narrow, just in your village only. You must broaden your horizons by obviously listening to radio for the county." While they generally liked and appreciated their immediate environment, any information needs were adequately fulfilled through the traditional primary contacts mentioned above – parish meetings, casual conversations, local shops and local newsletters. In Devon, the epicentre of interest was at Exeter, while in Penarth it was Cardiff and in Staffordshire Birmingham. One woman living some way from Cardiff said of a very localised station: "I don't think that would work because it's nice to know what is happening in Cardiff. If we want anything special we go there; we know Cardiff as well as we know Penarth." The main centres were sufficiently distant for local residents not to know enough about what was happening there, but sufficiently close for them both to want and need to know. Those living in major cities, and especially in the Capital, are perhaps prone to forget that most towns and cities in the UK have a very definable identity not only for the indigenous population but for those in the environs too.

The prospect of localised information was interpreted more as intrusive gossip, which could be had in more surreptitious circumstances in local shops, rather than a valuable service to the community; as a Leeds woman put it: "I really don't want to know what new curtains Mrs X has got." A different perspective on the limited and potentially irritating nature of very local stations was expressed by a Leeds woman: "You'd get the same people who enjoy phoning in or talking." A similar sentiment came in more graphic form from a Midlands man: "It can be a good thing or a bad thing. You do have certain people in Streetleigh who are on committees for every bloody thing. You always have the pushers and the do-gooders and the up-standing characters who don't do a damn thing except self-aggrandisement."

Some discussants cast doubt on whether people would listen to very local stations however relevant they were: "Community radio strikes me as a good idea but personally I tend to listen to the radio for music." The recognition implicit in this statement, that such stations could only derive their distinctive character from a speech-based format, represents a paradox: the *raison d'être* of these stations is itself the root of their unpopularity with many of the group discussants.

Reactions were not universally negative, and a theoretical distinction emerged between a local station which provided local listeners with a focus for identification with the local area and one which attempted to *create* a community feeling where none existed. A Swansea woman expressed the sense of identity reflected by the local station: "Before they ever had Swansea Sound your main radio stations never mentioned Swansea, Cardiff, Wales at all. . . . Once the local radio came in, it was ours – we had a part of it." A participant in a small Devon village made the contrast with a non-existent community: "It's just not a community if you have got to have a radio to make community spirit." Associations between people, which have not evolved through shared experiences, cannot be mechanistically contrived through radio. Thus, discussants in Newbury reflected sadly on the more transitional nature of the town's population now that the M4 had moved it closer to an outer London suburb: "They altered the face . . . of Newbury. People come in and move out. You have this sort of floating community, a sort of stepping-stone." It was clear that the old-established sense of stable community had been irrevocably disrupted, and that no amount of local stations could dismantle the motorway or lower house prices. The only role which a very local station could define for itself would be more akin to a social service.

The problem with any discussion on the role of or demand for local stations is that not only circumstances but also definitions will vary from area to area. Some attempt to collect standardised data was made in the national survey, but is subject to the qualification that any explanations incorporated into a question cannot eradicate different interpretations. With this limitation in mind, the question asked nationwide to tap the demand for small or "neighbourhood" stations tended to confirm the evidence from discussion groups: some support for a station dedicated to the *whole* of a town or city area, but more limited support for something on a more localised basis. Nearly half said they *would* like to see a neighbourhood station set up "in this area", given the definition of "a radio station that is run by local people with entertainment and news about the local area". A further 12% were undecided. Those who expressed positive interest were questioned as to how much they felt their area needed such a station: overall 29% said a little and 17% said a lot. Figure 7.1 shows how responses were distributed amongst the whole sample and compares the total with those living in cities.

The comparative lack of demand in cities is almost certainly an illustration of how the question can be subject to different interpretations in different areas. We have seen that the concept of neighbourhood is more alien to city dwellers, and hence the question will necessarily have less meaning. At the other end, however, there is a slightly stronger demand for local stations than overall, which is an understandable reflection of the city paradox: there are a number of areas with more close-knit communities who would benefit and enjoy some kind of more local station.

The next question, asked of those who wanted a neighbourhood station, provides the perspective mentioned earlier: stations which set their parameters beyond the narrow confines of the immediate environs have far more popular support than those of a more localised nature. Those living in towns or cities were asked whether the putative station should concentrate on their particular area or the whole of the town/city; those living in rural areas were asked whether it should

Figure 7.1
Demand for Neighbourhood Stations overall and within cities

	TOTAL	CITIES
Base	997	122
Need a lot	17%	20%
Need a little	29%	22%
Not needed	42%	52%
Don't know	12%	6%

Figure 7.2
Where Neighbourhood Stations should concentrate – by Locality

	TOTAL	CITY	SUBURB	LARGE TOWN	SMALL TOWN	RURAL
Base	580	60	140	78	100	210
Whole town/wider area	80%	66%	55%	90%	76%	70%
Just part/very small area	15%	32%	30%	5%	9%	18%
Don't know	5%	1%	15%	5%	15%	12%

concentrate on an area within a five mile radius or should be spread wider. With the exception of rural areas, Figure 7.2 is a quantified representation of the findings elaborated on earlier from discussion groups.

Overall, four out of five respondents define their own preference for a neighbourhood station as one that extends beyond the immediate locality. The small subsample of city dwellers qualifies the validity of the findings for that particular group, but these data are perfectly consistent with the qualitative analysis above. Inhabitants of towns are generally not interested in the perceived parochial nature of small stations, while those in cities and suburbs are more ambivalent. The figures for rural inhabitants are less easily explained, and may indicate latent support within some rural communities for a station linking several neighbouring villages rather than one for the immediate area only. Again, there are interpretational difficulties created by different definitions within different regions. In order to give the complete picture Figure 7.3 puts the question of neighbourhood stations in the context of the total national sample.

While the Figure below represents the qualified appeal of neighbourhood stations for listeners overall, the two ethnic surveys demonstrate more positive responses. Amongst Asians, 58% wanted a local neighbourhood station and a further 20% could not say. Amongst Afro-Caribbeans, the support was even stronger – 77% wanted a neighbourhood station, of whom over half thought the area needed it "a lot". A more specific question aimed at establishing attitudes of ethnic

Figure 7.3
Overall demand for Neighbourhood Stations

(Base = 997)

Don't want a neighbourhood radio station	42%
Want a neighbourhood station covering whole town/wider area	42%
Want a neighbourhood station covering just part/5 mile radius	10%
Want a neighbourhood station but don't know how extensive	6%

Figure 7.4
"In general do you think it would be a good idea or a bad idea for the Black/Asian community to have its own local radio station in this area?"

		ASIANS	AFRO-CARIBBEANS
	Base	71	73
Very good idea		48%	48%
Fairly good idea		18%	27%
Fairly bad idea		11%	8%
Very bad idea		4%	7%
Don't Know		13%	10%

groups towards their own local stations demonstrates fairly similar levels of enthusiasm. As Figure 7.4 shows, nearly half of both groups think such stations would be a very good idea; only around one in six responded negatively.

Responses to the final question in the series on neighbourhood stations are summarised in Figure 7.5. This question was designed to assess the level of enthusiasm for participation – either in administration or in making programmes; again, it was asked only of those who had supported the creation of such stations. The responses to questions such as these should not be interpreted as anything more than an approximation, since interviewees are notoriously prone to volunteer themselves for anything which can be safely forgotten the moment the interviewer leaves the living-room. The answers can be taken as a rough comparative guide, demonstrating that there would probably be more volunteers for occasional programme-making than anything on a more regular basis. Qualified as conclusions should be, there is certainly evidence of some disposition towards active participation in radio stations. It will come as little surprise that such willingness there is manifests itself especially amongst the young and city dwellers.

It might be expected that the greater enthusiasm expressed by the ethnic groups for their own local stations would be reflected in a greater degree of voluntary involvement in their running. While this is certainly true for the Afro-Caribbean community, the Asian responses were closer to the national sample (Figure 7.6).

Figure 7.5
Would personally like to be involved in . . .

			(Base = 549)
	YES	NO	DON'T KNOW
Running the station	18%	80%	2%
Helping make occasional programmes	33%	65%	2%
Helping make programmes regularly	15%	83%	2%

Figure 7.6
Involvement of Ethnic Groups in running stations: would personally like to be involved in . . .

		ASIANS			AFRO-CARIBBEANS		
Base		55			55		
		Yes	No	DK	Yes	No	DK
Running the station		24%	58%	15%	41%	52%	5%
Helping make occasional progs		36%	45%	18%	51%	42%	5%
Helping make progs regularly		25%	55%	16%	32%	63%	4%

While the positive responses of Asians are equivalent to the national sample, they were also less likely to be negative. Not only should the small base sizes encourage caution in interpretation, but it is always difficult to predict how much such hypothetical assistance would be translated into practice.

The insoluble question for small stations is, of course, whether they will attract sufficient numbers of listeners to render them viable. No research can answer a question of that complexity, but there are certainly some cautionary tales from reactions to the output from existing local radio stations. This chapter therefore concludes with an examination of some of the negative evaluations, given in both discussion groups and survey, of the current local radio services. While recognising that many of the new services will be qualitatively different from existing patterns of local radio, this study would be incomplete without some identification of the complaints and worries which listeners expressed about local radio. These may broadly and conveniently be defined as the "three As" – ads, accents and amateurism. Attitudes to commercials is dealt with in the following chapter, but the second and third complaints require some elaboration.

The charge of amateurism which emerged from several discussions, and was confirmed by the survey, is perhaps the most germane to the successful evolution of new local radio services (with the proviso that amongst Afro-Caribbean listeners, as we have seen, amateurism can represent a refreshing approach and a positive virtue). The BBC, through its long history in national radio, has developed a reputation for professionalism which many listeners believe to be lacking from commercial stations. This is not a complaint rooted in the past, a nostalgic longing for example for the news to be read in full evening dress, but a contemporary comparison made with existing national output. In several discussion groups, local radio was accused of being "amateurish", suburban or narrow, lacking in good personalities and presenters; commercial radio in particular was subject to criticism in overt comparison to the BBC national networks. A Glasgow man was quite explicit when asked if he would be likely to listen to a very local station: "I doubt it very much – I think I like to listen to professionals." One Leeds ILR listener was more ambivalent: "I do find them a bit amateur but I like the sort of newness that you feel they've got." It must be said that some of these complaints were not confined to commercial radio; another Leeds woman was equally explicit about Radio Leeds: "Local radio tends to sound very amateurish; it's possibly part of the ethos of local radio anyway but they tend to mix everything in together." A Swansea woman remembered tuning in to her ILR station and hearing an old school acquaintance with minimal experience doing a programme: "Some of these interviews are so unprofessional, the way [the presenters] do it." Another compared her own experience of local radio with what she regarded as the far more professional output of Capital in London: "You don't have people selling rotary cultivators and their wellies and things like that."

The more scientific approach of the survey confirms that, once those who express no opinion are excluded, over half of those interviewed agreed with the proposition that the national BBC is more professional than commercial radio – subject to some very illuminating age differences:

Figure 7.7
"Commercial radio is less professional than BBC national radio."

	TOTAL	15-24	25-34	35-44	45-54	55-64	65+
Base	821	177	144	145	112	93	141
Definitely agree	14%	6%	7%	16%	18%	18%	22%
Tend to agree	39%	34%	40%	41%	48%	43%	36%
Neither	14%	19%	8%	13%	11%	16%	15%
Tend to disagree	24%	31%	31%	21%	16%	18%	29%
Definitely disagree	9%	11%	14%	9%	7%	4%	7%

While a majority of the total clearly agree with this statement, opinion among the youngest age group is evenly divided. Furthermore, it is the older generations, raised on BBC style and presentation who are increasingly liable to agree as they get older. It is almost certain that many of these older listeners will have listened to very little, if any, commercial radio and their judgement may be tainted with an unjustified prejudice. The fact remains, however, that even among ILR's target age group – the 15–34s – a substantial proportion at least tend to agree. Even the most favourable comparison, amongst those whose favourite station is ILR, only diminishes the scale of the criticism rather than eliminating it. Nearly a quarter of ILR devotees agreed with the charge of amateurism, and one in five would not commit themselves;

well over half disagreed, which must be less than expected for a group with a self-confessed dedication to commercial radio.

Complaints about accents, though bound in with the problem of amateurism, were separate from it. Listeners were unimpressed by the rendering of their own local dialect, feeling it to be false, patronising and utterly inappropriate for the medium. One Welsh woman deprecatingly described local presenters as having "local yokel" accents. News in a local accent was definitely not appreciated: "I don't think you can trust the news so much if it's in a local accent." Just as one would not expect a BBC announcer to mimic the local accent, the credibility of any professional radio presenter is undermined if they cannot "speak properly." One Irish discussant said of the local presenter's accent: "It embarrasses you sometimes . . . you think, how did they get that job?" Scottish listeners were equally impatient with the broad Scottish accent on local radio: "That's why I don't listen to Radio Clyde – I feel embarrassed, the way that they talk . . . they are so Glaswegian. They don't talk like that in real life." In other words, these programmes reinforce the very stereotyped image which many listeners are trying to escape: "People in Glasgow and Scotland complain about the English media view of Scottish people, but a lot of Scottish programmes on radio . . . perpetuate the risk."

Similar sentiments were echoed around different regions of England, where attachment to local accent was clearly not extendable to the media; a Devon woman, who regarded her own accent as part of her heritage, did not want it overdone: "I wouldn't like to hear too broad [an accent] on the radio. I think it is accentuated sometimes when you pick the farmer with his bit of straw in his hair. . . . I don't think we want that." Returning to Wales, a question on attitudes to advertising evoked an unsolicited criticism which demonstrates that it is not only local presenters who can offend: "They have the same ones over and over again . . . really over the top Welsh accents. It is as if they are not Welsh people putting on Welsh accents . . . it does sound out of place."

Whatever the nature and strength of these objections, many listeners nevertheless continued to listen. If expansion of new and even more localised stations is to succeed, some measure of the numbers of listeners who found these problems intolerable is required. The responses to one question from the survey allow us to assess quite how terminal these objections might prove.

Around half the sample said they did not currently listen to commercial radio, and were asked if they had ever done so: six out of ten said that they had – which can be extrapolated to 30% of the population who have tried commercial radio but for some reason not continued with it. The unprompted reasons for giving it up are instructive, and suggest that any charges of amateurism are not instrumental in leading the retreat. The most commonly-stated objection, by just over one in five, was the advertisements; one in six said simply that they preferred another station, and the same proportion said the commercial station was just too boring or unappealing; just over one in ten gave the response which smacked of accusations of amateurism – that the station was badly presented or they disliked the style. This suggests that the greatest obstacle to the success of new stations is more likely to come from their most important source of funding than from any aversion to the style and nature of presentation.

CHAPTER 8

In Business: Attitudes to Commercial Forms of Funding Radio

Reference has been made more than once to the deep-seated BBC tradition of radio. It is hardly surprising that with a fifty-year start over its commercial counterpart, the Corporation has established certain yardsticks in listeners' minds for what constitutes acceptable radio. It is perhaps a tribute to the perseverance and quality of the independent sector that it has achieved its current share and status, given the national presence of and loyalty to the BBC. The total domination of BBC radio for so long has not only influenced listeners' perceptions of what constitutes an acceptable accent for professional broadcasters; it has also had a measurable bearing on tolerance of radio advertising. Commercials may constitute the life-blood of an expanding independent sector, but listeners often expressed exasperation with what they felt were generally boring and repetitive interruptions.

Advertising on radio was irritating in itself, but much more so when compared with television where advertising was perceived as better executed and more enjoyable. Comparing TV commercials with those on foreign channels, one woman thought they were "done very nicely", while another positively enjoyed them: "I can put up with them on telly because being visual some of them are amusing. Some of them are better than the programmes." By contrast the less powerful medium was obliged to compensate for its lack of immediate impact: "They have to be brash to get at you; they haven't got the visual, so they have got to blare out at you and that makes them doubly annoying." The vast majority compared radio unfavourably with TV, one discussant summarising perhaps the inherent disadvantage which afflicts commercial radio: "We've got the best advertising in the world, the advertising on telly – they've got the professionals to do the job, but on local radio it's a dead flop." Again: "When it comes on radio you just don't want to know because we have got so used to professionalism."

This time, commercial radio is accused of amateurism not through an unflattering comparison with the BBC, but with the unquestionably superior standards established by commercial television. These objections should not be underestimated, as a quantitative comparison with television demonstrates. While well over half of viewers find TV commercials enjoyable at least sometimes, the same can be said of only just over 40% of commercial radio listeners (Figure 8.1). These figures almost certainly underestimate the magnitude of difference between the two media, since the figures for radio must of necessity exclude those who never listen to ILR. A self-selected group of natural opponents to commercial radio, whose responses are certain to be overwhelmingly negative, is therefore disqualified from the comparison; as a consequence, reactions to commercial radio are shown in the best possible light.

It is hard to know whether radio advertising is simply creatively lacking in some absolute sense or suffers from the excellence of TV commercials. Certainly, the impact of new national commercial stations should help: commercial radio in the UK has attained an unwelcome reputation as the "two per cent medium", representing its share of the total advertising spend in stark contrast to the 8%, 10% or 12% shares regularly achieved in other countries. The limited money available is reflected in the limited creative talent which commercial radio attracts, and most advertising agencies will concede that there is little money and a good deal less kudos in creating the definitively "great" radio advertisement. The introduction of network commercial radio should attract some proportion of the national advertising budgets currently going to ITV and the national press, thereby facilitating a greater investment in the production of "enjoyable" commercials. The evidence from both survey and discussion groups is that the British viewer has developed a sophisticated taste in commercials, and expects the same manifestation of flair and ingenuity on radio as on television. The creative conundrum is even greater in radio, where the breaks are less clearly delineated and are much more an innate part of the programme;

Figure 8.1
"How often do you enjoy the advertisements when you listen to commercial radio/on television?"

		RADIO	TELEVISION
	Base	491	986
Always (4)		3%	5%
Often (3)		9%	16%
Sometimes (2)		29%	35%
Occasionally (1)		26%	28%
Never (0)		32%	15%
No answer		1%	1%
Never watch ITV		—	1%
Mean		1.3	1.7

Figure 8.2
"I would enjoy commercial radio/ITV more if it wasn't for the ads." (Bases exclude "Don't knows")

		RADIO	TELEVISION
Base		886	969
Definitely agree		14%	16%
Tend to agree		35%	36%
Neither		14%	14%
Tend to disagree		26%	26%
Definitely disagree		11%	8%

greater attention may need to be paid, especially on commercial music programmes, to ensure that the ads somehow maintain the pace and rhythm of the programme.

The enjoyment which can be derived from well-executed, unintrusive radio commercials was illustrated by two listeners of Capital: "They are just like the adverts on the television, sort of sing along to them like you do to the records"; "You listen to various commercial stations, and I think a lot of the ads they have on stations like Capital are highly amusing; a commercial break in Capital doesn't worry me. It's the soap powder commercials on television that just drive me to drink."

Whether antagonism towards radio commercials and the relative lack of "enjoyment" is a barrier to the appreciation of programmes is difficult to establish, since any measurement must by definition exclude those who never listen to commercial radio (quite possibly because they hate the ads!). Figure 8.2 suggests only that commercials do tend to interfere with enjoyment of radio programmes, but that the extent of that interference is no different from that experienced by those watching commercial television. Whether the distaste for commercials limits independent radio's ability to extend its appeal beyond its current audiences, is a theoretical question which this research cannot address.

Because radio commercials are not generally enjoyable, they can be both irritating and intrusive. The listener becomes an unwilling prisoner to a sound he or she finds objectionable: "When they come on television you can do something, make a cup of tea; on radio, you can't." Not only are they intrinsically tedious, but the problem is compounded when the tedium is repeated: "It's just stupid voices, it's so repetitive as well"; "It's like two year olds talking to you"; "I thought somebody had gone completely bananas or something, it sounded so childish"; "Adverts on radio annoy me more than on telly, they are more frequent"; "They get on your wick after a while"; "You might be getting them every five minutes whereas on TV it's every twenty."

Once again, it is impossible to escape the pervasive influence of the

Figure 8.3
"How often do you find the advertisements on the radio/on television annoying?"

		RADIO	TELEVISION
	Base	491	986
Always		16%	7%
Often		26%	25%
Sometimes		20%	28%
Occasionally		19%	24%
Never		18%	15%
No answer		1%	1%
Never watch ITV		—	1%
Mean		2.0	1.8

British tradition of television advertising, in this case the limits imposed on frequency. It is quite plausible that the moderation which ITV companies are obliged to observe during prime-time television plays some part in lowering listeners' threshold of the quantity of advertising which they are prepared to tolerate from the radio. The constraints imposed by the IBA may be less severe, but standards for the listener have already been defined by their exposure to more limited television advertising. Once again, the quantified data supports these conclusions, as Figure 8.3 demonstrates, but again the biased nature of the analysis base for listeners of commercial radio tends to minimise the scale of the differences. If non-ILR listeners were included, the levels of annoyance provoked by radio advertising would probably rise considerably. The same reservation applies to Figure 8.4 which compares responses to the number of commercials on radio and television. Perhaps the more interesting observation from this figure is the majority who feel that even the present levels of TV advertising are too high; little wonder, then, that the problem of quantity should be even more pronounced on radio.

Irritation was a function not only of the ads themselves but, as was

Figure 8.4
"Do you think there are too many advertisements on the radio/television?"

		RADIO	TELEVISION
	Base	491	986
Yes		54%	51%
No		36%	28%
No answer		10%	21%

Figure 8.5
"Advertisements are good for breaking up the monotony of radio."

(Bases exclude "Don't knows")

	TOTAL	ILR = FAVOURITE STATION
Base	900	194
Definitely agree	1%	4%
Tend to agree	17%	21%
Neither	19%	24%
Tend to disagree	36%	35%
Definitely disagree	27%	16%

implied by the earlier quotes, by the very nature of the medium which allowed for no respite. The very qualities of flexibility and intimacy which make the radio such a reliable and rewarding companion are those which render the advertisements so intrusive. The notion that continuous radio requires something different to break up the monotony is not accepted by British audiences, as respondents demonstrated in their overwhelming opposition to such a proposition. This sentiment does not even find favour with listeners who prefer ILR to other stations – Figure 8.5 shows them to be only a little less opposed to this statement than the overall total of nearly two-thirds.

Radio commercials, therefore, are not welcome breaks and if listeners wish to stay with the station they have to learn some way of coping with the intrusion. Many have: "It really goes over my head. I sort of block off as soon as I hear them"; "The adverts do drive me round the twist but I've got the knack of just switching off in my mind"; "They go in one ear and out the other." Some were philosophical and took their cue from the television experience: "I think we've come to live with ads on TV, so I think you could live with them – it's something you would get used to." For one or two, the knowledge that a commercial station's existence depended on the interruptions mitigated the damage: "I say to myself, well they have to put them on because that's the way they get their money"; or a little more bluntly: "They are a pain in the arse but they pay for the programme."

While one or two found radio commercials positively enjoyable, they represented for most a "necessary evil"; for a few, they were simply intolerable. The continuing need for channels without advertising, almost regardless of content, was emphasised more than once – especially in comparison to countries like Australia where radio is "just full of commercials – it spoils the listening"; and the US where "you get more commercials than you get programmes." Some listeners would simply abandon their radios: "To be honest I would seriously consider

86

dumping the lot if I had adverts on every single channel." Similarly, another listener was concerned that the BBC's role should continue: "I'm not saying every programme on the BBC is good, but I don't want every channel commercialised. I would like one, at least one channel where I wouldn't have to listen to adverts." It was evident that these listeners were referring not just to a national radio presence, but to a local presence as well. Chapter 10 looks in more detail at support for the BBC's role, but at this stage it should be observed that – speech content and adequate local news coverage aside – the definition of consumer choice is categorically interpreted by some listeners as the choice to listen to both local and national radio without unwelcome interruptions for commercials.

There is, however, one redeeming feature. In one respect alone, radio commercials provide a service which was acknowledged by a few discussants and by one group in particular in the survey. The role which local advertisements can play in providing valuable information about the available goods and services to the local population was recognised: "They tell you about local adverts, not things that are miles away"; "I like the local ones; they keep you in touch"; "These one-day sales, you wouldn't know about them unless you've got the radio on first thing in the morning." One even introduced a nationalist element: "Scottish things are advertised, and that's quite good because it's helping Scotland."

Participants in the Asian groups applied similar logic, and saw the commercial value of small-scale local advertising to local Asian communities: "The Asian people would like to advertise their own national products or whatever else they are selling . . . there is plenty of Indian business in Southampton, but they can't advertise Patna rice or whatever on Radio Solent; if there was an Asian programme that would fit in better." This was pursued in the same group: "These ads would be different because the products would concern you or your household – things you would be interested in." There would, in other words, be a convenient convergence of both specifically ethnic commercial information needs and commercial self-interest in helping businesses reach a very important target group at relatively cheap advertising rates. The benefits to both local community and local commerce were sufficiently attractive to overcome resistance to the innately lacklustre and disruptive nature of the advertisements themselves. It has to be said that no equivalent recognition of the possible benefits of local advertising was forthcoming from non-ethnic groups, and it is possible that very local stations planning to derive all their income from retail advertisers may find audiences resistant to the necessarily prosaic style of advertising involved.

Figure 8.6
"How often do you find the advertisements on the radio/on television informative?"

		RADIO	TELEVISION
	Base	491	986
Always		2%	2%
Often		13%	11%
Sometimes		29%	32%
Never		22%	21%
No answer		2%	1%
Never watch ITV		—	1%
Mean		1.4	1.4

Confirmation of the relative value placed upon the information function of radio commercials comes from the survey. Although the majority claim to find ads informative only occasionally or never, the proportions who find them informative at least sometimes are not insignificant and are almost exactly on a par with television.

Advertisers may, however, be interested in one key target group who seem to be more likely to find radio informative than television – which may in turn have implications for the amount of money they are prepared to commit. Although the subsample size suggests this should be treated with caution, housewives are apparently more amenable to radio messages than television.

Any explanation for this finding can be no more than speculative at this stage. It may be attributable to the more immediate relevance of messages during the day when advertised products can be purchased immediately. By contrast, for all the greater potency of the television

Figure 8.7
Information value of Radio Ads v TV Ads for Housewives

		RADIO	TELEVISION
	Base	68	164
Always		6%	4%
Often		19%	11%
Sometimes		31%	33%
Occasionally		21%	28%
Never		18%	21%
No answer		6%	1%
Never watch ITV		—	2%
Mean		1.7	1.5

message, no purchase will be made until the following day. It may be attributable to a different type of advertising on radio, tailored to suit the available audience, and therefore less likely to pursue the corporate image type of commercial which will have no immediate purchasing implications. Either way, it does represent an opportunity which could be exploited by new and existing commercial stations which they may want to pursue with further research.

Chapters 4 and 5 explored the reactions of listeners to advertising and ˈsponsorship within different programme genres. It was clear then that attitudes are not consistent across all programming strands, and the survival of new stations wholly reliant on advertising revenue will almost certainly depend as much on their sensitivity to listener reservations about radio commercials as on the content of the programmes themselves. Anecdotal evidence on the distinctions drawn between ads in speech-based programming and ads in music programmes will illustrate the differences.

The quarrel with ads for music lovers is their tendency to interrupt the flow of music. "I like listening to continuous music, I don't really like the adverts", said one young man while another made an explicit comparison with his local ILR station: "If it's Radio 1 you can listen to it continuously without it distracting you." Again, radio compares unfavourably with television: "With the telly they're supposed to bring the adverts on during a natural break, whereas [on] the radio a bloke will be playing a record and half way through it stops and he starts giving an advert." A fan of ILR's network Chart show responded similarly: "They cut them up . . . in midstream, they don't wait till they have finished." Whatever the truth of advertising on music radio, the perception is of unwarranted and undesirable interruptions of good music. The references to 'continuous music' seem to be inherited from a previous attachment to BBC Radio 1 which of course has never been tainted with commercial breaks. The establishment of pop radio in 1967, seven years before the first commercial stations were introduced, almost certainly helped to breed a generation of young listeners accustomed to an unbroken flow of DJ and music. The legacy is an audience which still feels uncomfortable with commercial interruptions, and may well continue to do so.

In a country with almost no tradition of commercials on speech-based stations (LBC constituting the major exception), it is no surprise that opposition to such an innovation was even more pronounced. "Worse if it's speech" was one comment which continued: "You can pick it up again with the music, but with speech you can't." One listener who enjoyed radio plays thought it would intrude on the privacy of the radio audience: "Can you imagine sitting in a chair, closing your eyes and listening to a play – and suddenly half way through a play you are trying to imagine, out comes some silly sod saying whatever he wants." Another agreed that plays would suffer: "I think the worst breaks would be in a play or something, it would put you right off." Someone else thought the consequences for comedy programmes would be undesirable: "They are doing *Hancocks Half Hour*, that ran for one hour and five minutes because they kept interrupting every three minutes with an advert; it didn't make sense at all." As reported earlier, breaks *between* programmes mitigated the strength of opposition: "If it's just at the beginning of a programme it's not so bad." For one or two, commercials between programmes even rendered them acceptable: "I have no objection to ads providing they put them on between programmes."

Attitudes were even more positive towards sponsorship, again as reported earlier, as long as it did not interrupt: "I wouldn't object to sponsorship at the beginning or end, that would be fine." Some even volunteered suggestions for suitable sponsors: "Shell could sponsor because Shell is sensible on the television"; and there was potential for local sponsorship which could be exploited: "You could get Newbould pies to sponsor" enthused one Northern listener, referring to a chain of local butchers.

Other forms of funding were summarily dismissed in most cases. Neither car radio licences nor subscription seemed to go down well, on the basis that "they" get enough from the licence fee and adverts to provide the service we want without coming to us for more. For similar reasons, re-introducing a radio licence would not prove popular: "I think we'd put up with advertising rather than have radio licences." Even for those who believed in radio as an intrinsic part of the community there was opposition to public money being spent on creating more stations. Rates were not an appropriate source of funding because it was not perceived as part of a local civic service: councils could barely afford their traditional obligations. The notion of more stations was supportable for most people only if those who wanted them were prepared to finance them; public subsidies were not popular.

CHAPTER 9

Science Now: Frequencies, Reception and the User-friendly Radio

It is one of the ironies of modern technology that amongst all the marvellous futuristic developments there is not yet a universal cure for the oldest technical problems: poor reception and interference on the simple little radio. Once again, of course, the essence of the problem lies in those very qualities which make radio so irresistible: inextricably tied to flexibility and mobility are variations in quality of reception and the risk of fading signals.

Whatever the perfectly legitimate technical explanations, it is certainly a puzzling and sometimes intensely frustrating conundrum for listeners. Reception is important, and attitudes must surely harden as the ear becomes increasingly attuned to the clarity not only of television signals but of high quality digital reproduction on music systems. Attitudes have changed since the fuzzy and barely audible sounds of the early radio transmissions. According to one discussant, clarity now is "very important. Can't stand listening [to radio] all crackly and half out of tune." A fellow listener echoed the incomprehension of many that such a simple problem defied solution in the modern age: "I don't think we should have to either these days with all the technology."

Night-time listening in particular suffers. One female listener enjoyed Radio 1 in the evening, but complained that "it goes and it keeps fading away into French." Again, from a rural listener: "Reception is terrible, absolutely terrible at night." Precise descriptions of the varieties of noise produced by late-night radio varied, but one listener attempted a graphical reproduction: "It's awful, and it's getting worse. You get wee-oo wee-oo."

The problem was exacerbated in some of the more rural parts of the country, and city listeners accustomed to strong signals throughout the day may be surprised by the feelings of anguish, frustration and annoyance expressed by listeners in both outlying areas and, sometimes, even in cities. A Glasgow listener complained: "We get a lot of interference because we've got high flats where I live. . . . It's difficult to get Radio 1 sometimes." Another in the more rural reaches of Devon described how the countryside made both house and car listening fairly unpredictable: "We have terrible problems here because of the lie of the land.

91

Figure 9.1
"I would listen to more radio if reception was better."

| | | TOTAL | 15–24 | CITY DWELLERS | Favourite Station | | | | | |
					R1	R2	R3	R4	BBC LR	ILR
	Base	997	201	122	242	141	22	123	95	199
Definitely agree (+2)		7%	11%	15%	9%	4%	5%	7%	5%	9%
Tend to agree (+1)		15%	21%	14%	17%	13%	14%	12%	20%	17%
Neither (0)		17%	18%	14%	21%	18%	9%	18%	13%	17%
Tend to disagree (−1)		32%	34%	29%	31%	33%	45%	32%	40%	36%
Definitely disagree (−2)		24%	13%	24%	19%	28%	23%	29%	18%	20%
Don't know		5%	2%	5%	3%	4%	5%	2%	4%	3%
Mean		−0.5	−0.2	−0.3	−0.4	−0.7	−0.7	−0.6	−0.5	−0.4

If you are driving in your car, you will lose it completely going down one lane and it will come back again in another." The implication of poor reception, even if only in isolated pockets, is a potentially smaller volume of listening. Figure 9.1 gives the responses to the question which attempts to quantify to what extent listening is diminished by poor reception; it is possibly higher than one might expect.

It is illuminating in itself that over one in five radio listeners would apparently listen more if reception were better. Even allowing for an over-eagerness in self-reporting, this figure suggests a pool of listening that FM stations may be able to tap. This would be less likely were these responses confined to rural areas where the more widespread populations would make such ventures a good deal more problematic. As Figure 9.1 shows, however, the greater listening potential seems to lie in the big city areas and, in particular, amongst the young of whom nearly a third claim that better reception would encourage them to listen more. This may be a reflection of greater intolerance of inferior signals amongst those brought up on high quality hi-fi sounds, or it may be increasing awareness of the benefits of FM. It may also be a reflection of weaker signals available in some regions for the two younger-profile stations, Radio 1 and ILR. It certainly implies some potentially unsatisfied demand in areas where good reception should not be a problem.

A question which asked which stations, if any, listeners ever found hard to receive because of interference or weak signals gives an idea of the scope of the problem. Figure 9.2 shows that Radio 1 comes top of the list with ILR close behind. These figures, however, are as much a reflection of the number of listeners each station tends to attract, and a better analysis is provided by the second column – those who have ever experienced reception problems on their own favourite station. This demonstrates some consistency, and the average proportion of around a quarter may be unexpectedly high. Given the scale of the problem, and the possibility that poor reception may be suppressing the volume of listening amongst the young, it may be less surprising that FM represents for many people a better alternative.

Figure 9.2
"Do you ever have difficulty in receiving clearly a station you want to listen to because of interference or a weak signal?"

		TOTAL	OWN FAVOURITE STATION
	Base	888	N/A
Radio 1		10%	27%
ILR		9%	26%
Radio 4		5%	26%
Radio 2		5%	24%
BBC LR		4%	21%

Figure 9.3
"Do you ever listen to the radio on VHF, which is also called FM?"

	TOTAL	AGE								CLASS			
		15-19	20-24	25-34	35-44	45-54	55-64	65-74	75+	AB	C1	C2	DE
Base	888	106	84	152	154	118	100	104	61	184	217	225	260
Yes	57%	72%	57%	64%	64%	50%	46%	45%	38%	69%	58%	56%	47%
No	35%	22%	35%	31%	28%	42%	43%	46%	48%	23%	37%	35%	43%
Don't Know	8%	7%	8%	5%	8%	8%	11%	9%	15%	8%	6%	8%	11%

Although many listeners in the discussion groups did not listen to FM (a few were unsure what the difference between the wavebands was), those who did were undoubtedly converts. The quality of the sound, the strength of the signal and the stereo capacity were recognised and appreciated for the extra dimension they added to radio listening. "I prefer FM normally, it's a better signal and you can get it in stereo" was one comment, while another had almost given up medium wave listening: "I prefer FM for the quality. I only tune in to medium wave if the channel I want isn't on FM." Music listening is enhanced for many listeners by the better quality sound on FM, and this applies to both classical and pop. One classical music fan in the Midlands was categorical about the detrimental effect of medium wave listening in his area: "The AM frequency would be too bad for Radio 3 music. If they gave it AM they might as well do away with Radio 3 total." A Preston teenager listened to the Radio 1 Chart show on FM "because it's a lot clearer." There is, of course, a less legitimate reason for deserting the inferior quality of the medium wave: "It's not all that good if you're trying to copy it."

It is not only appreciation of music on radio which FM assists: speech radio fans also enjoy the greater clarity as well as the stereo capability. Plays, in particular, were singled out as benefiting from FM transmission: "A play comes out better on FM than it does on medium wave." It was not only the better quality of sound, but the times at which plays are often scheduled: "You get a better clarity and also plays are generally on in the evening, and medium wave reception in the evening is worse."

Any attempt to quantify FM listening through self-reporting by listeners, as the broadcasters themselves have consistently found, is subject to error based on widespread ignorance about the differences between the wavebands. The survey questions should, therefore, be regarded as no more than an approximation of how listening behaviour takes place, and where there tends to be the greatest interference. Overall, Figure 9.3 demonstrates that over half the sample claimed to have listened to FM radio at some stage, in particular the 15–19 age group. The same figure also reflects significant class differences which may have implications for the BBC's publicity programme as it gradually moves all services on to FM.

At this stage of frequency development, FM listening is likely to be as much a reflection of which stations have moved permanently to FM transmission and what proportion of the country is covered by the signal. When analysed in terms of listeners' favourite stations (Figure 9.4), a clearer pattern emerges which differentiates between Radio 2 and other national stations, as well as between BBC and commercial

Figure 9.4
Whether Listen to FM – by Favourite Station

		TOTAL	R1	R2	R3	R4	BBC LR	ILR
							Favourite Station	
	Base	888	223	136	22	121	92	191
Yes		57%	52%	44%	95%	64%	62%	69%
No		35%	41%	49%	5%	31%	32%	23%
Don't know		8%	8%	7%	–	5%	7%	9%

local radio. This may reflect a less widely available signal, but may equally reflect a greater resistance amongst Radio 2 and BBC local radio listeners to listen on FM – almost certainly a result of the older listener profiles of both these stations.

Resistance to appeals directed at persuading listeners to forsake their accustomed position on the dial for another which would enable the same station to be received with improved sound quality, is a difficult concept to grasp until faced with irrefutable proof of the innate conservatism (and in some cases fear) of the radio listener. Some listeners would go to almost any length to avoid the trauma of having somehow to adjust the tuning dial on their sets, although the self-confessions were accompanied by some embarrassment: "I don't retune – I have got two wirelesses in my kitchen. I know it sounds daft, but I have one for Mercia Sound and one for Radio 4 . . . I don't like retuning." Children are the worst enemy, constantly infiltrating the inner sanctum of kitchen or bathroom and inflicting the worst possible sabotage on the unsuspecting adult: "If they mess around with it, and you switch it on in the morning . . . I'm there for ages then. Something popular comes on, you think it must be Radio 1, and all of a sudden you get *Recipe for the Day*"; "My daughter comes down and they tune my wireless into Radio 4 and then when they go home I have a heck of a job to get back where I want to be." The children, more technically adept and often with little sympathy for the parental dilemma, are unrepentant: "My mum usually has it on Radio Lancashire when I go downstairs in the morning, so I turn it on to Radio 1."

This reluctance to surrender the security of the familiar position on the tuning dial has direct implications for programme choice: in a rather bizarre reverse application of the theory of technological determinism, many radio listeners are virtually prisoners to their own technological fears. It is not an exaggeration to state that the conservatism of listening choice is to some extent determined by the perceived difficulties of relocating the most favoured station. One Radio 2 listener said: "I have a job to find Radio 2 and I won't go on to another station because I have such a job to find that one. Once I have it, I stay."

While fear is a factor, and tended to be expressed more by older listeners in the discussion groups, it has to be said that laziness also contributes to this innate conservatism. Some listeners who acknowledge the existence of potentially interesting and worthwhile programmes on other stations, prefer to stick with their familiar favourite: "It's too much effort to remember when programmes are on . . . I would much rather put Radio 1 on because I know that I am going to be able to listen to it." The effort involved in planning radio listening is in stark contrast to the time and energy often expended in planning an evening's television viewing. One listener was aware of individual programmes through her husband, but could not share his patience in actually looking up their transmission times: "He will look it up whereas I don't, I am too lazy. I just like to turn, to switch on and be able to listen to something all day without it getting on my nerves."

Listening behaviour, therefore, is not only a product of life-style and cultural preferences, but is structured by technical limitations: both fear and laziness inhibit experimentation amongst radio listeners who might otherwise be quite willing to try new types of programmes. A few are prepared to expose themselves to the occasional challenge: "Late at night I go round all the stations and it's all foreigners or loud music. I don't know what station I'm on, I just turn them over." The more circumspect will only try it when they know there is a safe route back: "It'll pass the time while you're sitting in the traffic, but what station it's on I haven't a clue. I just press my buttons and I've forgotten what I end up with." Night-time and car listening were the most frequent times for adventure, but even that became too frustrating for some: "I find at night there are so many stations that you just get buzzing in your ears. I just gave it up and went back to Radio 1."

The rewards for such flights of fancy can be considerable, and several listeners were delighted by the unexpected pleasures of stations which had been disregarded: "I was really shocked – it was only about three months ago that I decided to flick through the channels and I heard some really good music on Radio 2." Knowing the identity of stations is not crucial to enjoyment. One man found himself unwittingly tuned to Radio 4 and described a programme he had thoroughly enjoyed: "6.30 on the way home from work – I don't know what station it was on but it was a comedy programme." There was considerable ignorance not just of the *identity* of programmes or stations, but of the *range* of stations and programming available. One young man described the pleasure he derived from a station which he had recently discovered: "I don't know what radio station it is. I just know where it actually is on the dial." The station, it transpired, was Radio 3.

Figure 9.5
"I would listen to more stations on radio if I had a push-button radio."

(Base = 997)

Definitely agree (+2)	3%
Tend to agree (+1)	14%
Neither (0)	19%
Tend to disagree (−1)	31%
Definitely disagree (−2)	27%
Don't know	5%

Given the sufficiency of range and choices which most listeners believe they are blessed with, do these technological limitations make any difference to people's listening diet – that is, given a simple means of retuning from station to station without inducing panic, would listeners make better use of more stations? Some of the reactions from older listeners in discussions suggested that, if television technology were applied to radio sets, they might: "It is much easier with a TV, just to push the knobs in than to mess about trying to find the programme you want with the radio." A push-button radio would encourage greater experimentation: "I would just switch until I discovered something I liked." Car drivers well versed in the technical advantages of pushing buttons needed no convincing: "That's why I find the car radio much easier to use than the radio in the house."

The survey, however, suggests that easier technical solutions may only affect the radio listening habits of a fairly small minority. Figure 9.5 shows that the majority, nearly six out of ten, do not think a push-button radio would make any difference to the number of stations they listen to, although one in six thinks it might. While this figure is small, it would still represent a considerable increase in the number of stations which listeners would sample overall.

A new generation of radio technology will not induce dramatic changes, despite the plea of one frustrated Welsh woman: "You would think with all the technology they have got that it would be more sensible, wouldn't you, like the television. That is nice and easy." In other words, the push-button radio may not have dramatic implications for listening behaviour but it would make many listeners a great deal happier: for something which has achieved such an intimate role in most people's lives, the user-friendly philosophy generally applied to computers would probably be more appropriate.

98

CHAPTER 10

The Public Service Philosophy in Radio

The public service concept as applied to television has undergone several examinations, explanations and interpretations over the years. Its application to radio, however, has been explored in less detail. Before examining whether the consequences of public service obligations are generally accepted or opposed by listeners, some framework for definition needs to be established.

From the outset, it must be emphasised that public service in its correct sense is not simply a synonym for the BBC. It encompasses a series of regulations and regulatory structures which place certain obligations of programming and advertising on the independent sector. The result, in this country, has been an independent broadcasting sector which is not solely concerned with the creation of profits but has been required to operate within the same values of range and quality as the BBC. These obligations have been adapted to suit the greater flexibility of radio, and need to be explained in more detail.

Conceptual distinctions are sometimes arbitrary but it is possible to identify six different strands of public service broadcasting with practical significance for radio: a) the system should provide a range of programmes to satisfy a variety of tastes; b) news and information should be an integral part of every station's output; c) news and factual reporting should be strictly impartial; d) all UK listeners should be able to receive radio wherever they choose to live; e) programmes should have due regard for standards and quality; f) there should be programmes for minorities who do not necessarily share either the ethnic background or cultural tastes of the majority of listeners.

The radical changes being proposed for the future of radio – involving a deregulation which will have major implications for the public service provision – will remove some of the statutory obligations which currently govern independent radio. In the light of these proposals, the commitment of those who pay for and listen to radio services to these elements of the public service philosophy is of instrumental interest in an expanding and deregulated competitive environment.

Despite the tendency of listeners to stay with one station and therefore one strand of programming, they appreciated the range available to those who want variety. The analogy with television is dangerous,

99

because national radio stations are not individually constrained to provide a range of output; the range is forthcoming from the *system* of four stations. Many were impressed by the range currently provided over four national stations, and expected the principle to be extended to the new national stations of the future: "If they are just going to put on Radio 1 music – which is a load of rubbish – they shouldn't bother to have three extra stations."

An extension of this concern for some listeners is the risk that unbridled competition may squeeze out the existing range. One listener explicitly acknowledged the role of the licence fee: "If you didn't pay the licence fee you wouldn't get some of the programmes because the advertisers wouldn't advertise on it." Drawing an analogy with Channel 4, another discussant suggested that the convergence effects of direct competition might be similar on radio: "They're probably going to sell their own advertising space and once they do that it will look a lot more similar to ITV." The variety available in libraries was quoted as another analogy: "It's like the library; if they only had the books that went out most, they would only have American novels." In other words, some listeners were afraid that supply might be determined by the most popular demand, thereby disenfranchising those whose tastes did not coincide with the majority.

Concern that range should not be sacrificed was translated into almost universal support for stations which catered for minority groups. Minorities, in this sense, were interpreted and described in the widest possible way: not just cultural and ethnic minorities, but minorities of taste, region and age. Some discussants displayed a sophisticated understanding of the financial complexities, and were worried that advertisers' desire to attract audiences with high disposable incomes might deprive less wealthy groups of their own tastes in radio. One was particularly brutal about the aspirations of ILR: "These stations are only there to make a profit. If they don't make a profit, they will do away with them. They are only there to make money, not for you and I."

The elderly, in particular, were regarded as vulnerable. Some discussants, while accepting that commercial radio was capable of offering a range of programmes, felt that it tended to constitute a medium for the younger generation: "They cater for the majority and the majority just now is teenagers and twenty year olds. From thirty down they all like this heavy metal and bash bash bash, tick tick tick and that seems to be the majority of programmes on radio now." Though an overstatement of current population trends, this was an interesting reflection both on the current image of commercial radio and on listeners' views of the direction which an expanding commercial sector might take.

100

Commitment to minority taste programmes was strong in both discussion groups and survey. Given the reluctance of most listeners to dip into any other station, least of all those catering for very specialist tastes like Radio 3, the strength of support was more remarkable for not being rooted in any self-interest. The listening needs of others were, quite explicitly, important: "Classical music is not my cup of tea . . . but it would be a sad day if we lost it. You've got to cover for minorities"; "The minority must be catered for." Even those who go nowhere near the specialist channel support its existence: "I don't think I've ever heard it, but I think it should be there if anyone wants it. It should be there for them." This commitment is reinforced by the survey findings:

Figure 10.1
"Specialist music stations like Radio 3 are a waste of licence-payer's money and should be replaced by something which appeals to more people."

		TOTAL	15–24
	Base	997	201
Definitely agree		3%	3%
Tend to agree		14%	20%
Neither		19%	23%
Tend to disagree		31%	35%
Definitely disagree		27%	17%
Don't know		5%	2%
Mean		−0.7	−0.4

The statement was strongly worded in a deliberate attempt to challenge the strength of commitment to programmes of a specialist nature. Despite the provocative nature of the question, the majority believed that stations of limited appeal should not be sacrificed to the majority cause. That this sentiment was espoused with less enthusiasm by the 15–19 age group is difficult to interpret: they may be deterred by the example of a station with specialist music of less specific appeal than, for example, contemporary specialist music. They may simply be displaying a greater self-interest than other age groups. Just possibly, these are the first signs of a fragmentation of the public service ethos in the younger generation, but such a far-reaching conclusion would require more research.

Overall, then, groups with different cultural tastes and different musical tastes should be catered for; the BBC was for some a rainbow coalition of taste, not simply pandering to the demands of the majority but prepared to offer quality programmes across the whole spectrum of musical and speech tastes. "Radio 4 pleases some, Radio 1 pleases some, and Radio 2 pleases me and other people. Radio 3 pleases a lot of

Figure 10.2

"Do you think commercial local stations should be allowed to have *no* news bulletins at all if they wish, or should they have to have *some* news bulletins?"

		TOTAL	BBC LR	ILR
			Favourite Station	
	Base	997	95	199
Can have none		16%	13%	14%
Must have some		72%	74%	77%
Don't know		6%	7%	3%
No answer		6%	6%	6%

people too but they are in the minority and that's what you pay your licence fee for – that's the way I look at it." The BBC is recognised as being all things to all listeners, the epitome of public service practice for which there is every sign of positive support and appreciation. "The BBC is to cater for everyone; someone who wants something serious that relaxes them should have something to turn to" was the accepted philosophy.

The existence of stations providing for minority tastes can have benefits for listeners other than the altruistic fulfilment of other people's tastes. One listener sometimes experimented with new programmes because "it might turn out to be very interesting". In other words, the availability of such output can assist in broadening cultural horizons by exposing listeners to music or speech programmes of which they have no experience. One Afro-Caribbean man described his experience of a chance exposure to Radio 3: "I despised classical music before, then I heard it once or twice and I thought – that sounds all right. Now I listen to mostly classical and soul and a bit of jazz." While speculative tuning was very much the exception during everyday listening, we have seen that listeners are over a period of time prepared to sample other stations; as tastes progress, access to a variety of different stations will enable people to realise new and developing interests through the radio.

Strict guidelines currently in operation oblige commercial stations to provide news bulletins on a regular basis. The rationale, to ensure that listeners are kept informed of national and international as well as local events, is not necessarily axiomatic; it is conceivable that this long-standing public service obligation may have become superfluous or even onerous for listeners.

In fact, nearly three-quarters of listeners support the obligation on commercial stations to provide *some* news bulletins and Figure 10.2 shows support to be even high amongst commercial radio fans.

It is difficult to interpret the scale of such support for inclusion of news content in all commercial stations. One factor is likely to be a somewhat conservative adherence to the status quo, but this alone is a simplistic interpretation. At the root of it may lie some kind of support for a notion of civic responsibility, the duty of all radio and television channels to keep their audience in touch with the world outside the immediate environment of home or car. The *basis* for such endorsement of compulsory news provision requires further research. Its existence is unambiguous.

Frequency of news bulletins, however, is a greater bone of contention, and many ILR listeners complained as bitterly about the dull repetition of news bulletins as about the advertisements: "The hourly news is a bit ridiculous, it's too much." The abbreviated nature renders it less interesting on an hourly basis: "It would be better to have news once or twice a day, but decent news." Many listeners, especially housewives, will be listening for large parts of the day and for them the hourly repetition is particularly tedious: "You hear it once, then it comes on every hour. It's news to somebody but to the people that are listening all day it's not news." Even those stations which specialise in news and current affairs do not escape criticism: an LBC listener complained: "If it's half past seven you get a bit of news, again at eight o'clock, you hear it again at half past eight and that drives you crazy." The greater ambivalence about the frequency of bulletins is reflected in Figure 10.3.

Those in favour of frequent bulletins are still in a majority, but only just. Amongst the teenage group, the majority is reversed and a greater proportion would prefer that stations be allowed to choose: a sign of the more parochial view of the world traditionally associated with teenagers. Again, both ILR and BBC local radio listeners are more likely to support regular and frequent bulletins on commercial stations than listeners in general. Whatever lighter touch is being counselled, there is less demand than might be expected amongst listeners for releasing

Figure 10.3
"At the moment commercial radio stations have to have regular and frequent news bulletins. Do you think this is a good idea or should the stations themselves be allowed to choose how many news bulletins they want to have?"

			Age		Favourite Station	
		TOTAL	15-19	20-24	BBC LR	ILR
	Base	997	109	92	95	199
Good idea		51%	39%	55%	59%	57%
Stations choose		41%	55%	39%	33%	38%
Don't know		9%	6%	5%	8%	5%

commercial stations from their present obligation to provide regular news coverage.

The public service tradition most deeply embedded in listeners' minds is the traditional requirement within broadcasting for unbiased and balanced reporting. The question put to respondents drew an analogy with the editorial freedom of the press; but the potential for a host of stations covering different shades of political opinion aroused very little sympathy; asked whether radio stations should be allowed to take sides or remain impartial, the vast majority were unwilling to surrender the impartiality of broadcast news for either the BBC or commercial radio:

Figure 10.4
"Newspapers can take a stand on an issue, and support one side of an argument, whereas television has to stay balanced between different sides. Do you think BBC radio/commercial radio should be able to take sides, or should it always be balanced?"

	BBC RADIO	COMMERCIAL RADIO
Base	997	997
Take sides	8%	11%
Be balanced	85%	81%
Don't know	7%	8%

One concept which is difficult to communicate is the differential economic cost of serving different parts of the country. It has become a fact of British broadcasting that even the remotest regions of Scotland and Wales can receive signals – at least from the BBC – for a flat-rate fee. Any attempt to challenge this philosophy in the discussion groups met with stiff resistance – there was no support for increasing the financial burden on those in the more distant outposts who were disproportionately expensive to reach. One discussant expressed the sort of imperial concern for Scottish Highlanders which gives Londoners a bad name: "I don't think they should pay more because they are unfortunate enough to live up there and we are living in London." The concern of most discussants was a little more generalised: "I don't think it's fair if people are penalised because of where they live." Aroused by the very suggestion of such an iniquity, one listener was driven to a caustic analogy: "It's the same as saying – you've got to pay more licence fee because your dog is bigger." The common theme which united these and other participants was a sense of national belonging, that the BBC in particular "belongs to the British people and doesn't belong to any government"; everyone should be allowed to participate in and derive satisfaction from this national resource. The notion applies across all ages and was captured by one teenager: "They should get the same amount from everybody. We're all part of the same United Kingdom and we're all getting the same service."

Although statements on universal reception tended to apply more to the BBC, the sentiments expressed within discussion groups which favoured the continuing tradition of a public service element in radio were not applied exclusively to any individual stations or broadcasters; they were statements of support for a certain presence in national life. In no sphere of the public service tradition was this more important than in the difficult and essentially intangible concept of *quality of programmes*. In discussion after discussion, whether addressing the superiority of Radio 4 drama, the comprehensiveness of Radio 2 sports coverage or the presentational style of Radio 1 DJs, listeners were keen to praise the essential *quality* of BBC programming. We have seen greater reservations expressed by some ILR listeners but even then the ability of commercial radio to represent and promote the interests of the local community was appreciated and applauded. Some criticised stations which did not conform to their own predilections; this should not be confused with poor quality engendered by the *system*, for which there was almost universal praise: "We have a very fine reputation throughout the world for the way we present our broadcasting and I think that ought to be clung on to."

Hand in hand with an appreciation of existing provision was a nervousness and apprehension about any changes which might in some way diminish the universal perception of quality. Quantity was not synonymous with quality and could even prove its antithesis: "I think if you start increasing the airwaves you're obviously going to start decreasing the quality of programmes." These expressions of concern were not only the natural conservatism of groups who, as we have seen, regard themselves as already adequately served; several listeners mentioned the frequent (and not always desirable) appearances by certain personalities in many different programmes: "You're spreading all the talent out and the talent's thin on the ground as it is." The upshot is a cautious and unenthusiastic approach from listeners to any additional choice which might serve to compromise a precious and valued commodity. Listeners do not interpret radio solely in terms of the one or two stations to which they devote most time, but as a total and integrated system for which the majority are grateful. Radical alterations which fail to take account of this complex interrelationship and which are perceived as damaging to any part of the system will probably be regarded as unnecessary and undesirable.

Perhaps the best illustration of listeners' application of traditional public service values to radio is in their attitudes to the old Reithian

Figure 10.5
"How much, if at all, do you think radio should aim to . . ."

		INFORM	ENTERTAIN	EDUCATE
	Base	997	997	997
A great deal		38%	56%	29%
A fair amount		43%	33%	41%
A little		10%	4%	18%
Not at all		1%	*	5%
Don't know		7%	7%	7%

trilogy. Radio should, certainly, provide a means of entertainment; for the great majority it should also deliver at least a fair amount of information and education.

These values are supported, but are applied to the system rather than individual stations. A further question asked whether every station, or just some, should have programmes which inform or educate. Over two-thirds were prepared to exclude stations from any public service mandate as long as there were some to uphold these standards overall.

Although majorities of all subgroups were more sympathetic to this systemic approach, it was social-grade classification which showed the most pronounced variations. The greater support amongst the more educated for an information and education element in every station probably reflects their own appetite for such programming, or maybe their opposition to purely entertainment-based stations. Whatever the subgroup variance, stations providing entertainment only are generally acceptable as long as the other two constituents of good broadcasting are present within the system.

While the public service responsibilities of the independent sector were recognised and appreciated by most listeners, it was scarcely surprising that the BBC should emerge as the standard-bearer of what constituted the best of radio. There was never any doubt that, whatever listeners' own preferences, continuation of existing BBC national

Figure 10.6
"Do you think every radio station should have some programmes which inform and educate people, or is it all right provided at least some do?"

		TOTAL	AB	C1	C2	DE
	Base	997	199	235	249	312
Every station		19%	32%	20%	13%	16%
At least some		70%	63%	73%	76%	69%
Don't know		5%	2%	4%	4%	7%
No answer		6%	4%	3%	6%	7%

services was an absolute precondition to the maintenance of a quality service. While this is not an area of policy debate, the BBC's contribution to *local* radio has not been a foregone conclusion. In the light of changes which could, as described in independent local radio, see a diminishing news and information content in independent local radio, equivalent services provided by BBC local radio take on a new significance. The presence of the Corporation in local radio at a time of fiscal constraint may have been under review, but it undoubtedly has the support of listeners:

Figure 10.7
"How important do you think it is for the BBC to provide local radio stations in most areas of the country?"

		TOTAL	SOUTH WEST	WEST MIDLANDS
	Base	997	100	113
Very important		27%	38%	18%
Fairly important		45%	49%	43%
Not very important		18%	8%	24%
Not at all important		6%	4%	8%
Don't know		4%	1%	7%
Mean		2.0	2.2	1.8

It may be described as qualified support, given the quarter who do not give positive responses, but most listeners are fairly convinced of the legitimate role of the BBC in local radio. Regional variations can reflect a myriad number of demographic and other factors, including the relative strengths and weaknesses of existing stations, and should be interpreted with caution; however, the great enthusiasm for BBC local radio in the South-West is an intriguing contrast to its more muted reception in the West Midlands. To some extent, but by no means all, this will be attributable to the lower penetration of ILR in the South-West Region – around 50% compared to 85% nationally. The West Midlands, on the other hand, boasts four commercial stations, while BBC local radio has not yet achieved wide coverage.

Approval for the BBC's role in local radio is subject to greater qualification when those listeners who feel it is important are offered a more difficult (though not strictly realistic) dilemma: given a fixed sum of money to be spent on either local or national radio, which should the BBC choose? This one is a split decision, and again Figure 10.8 illustrates that the overall responses are subject to significant variations in the social-grade subgroups.

Figure 10.8
"If the BBC had a fixed sum of money, which it could spend *either* on local radio or on improving the national radio service, which would you prefer?"

(Base = All who think it important that BBC should provide local radio stations)

		TOTAL	Class			
			AB	C1	C2	DE
	Base	713	150	167	175	221
Local		45%	31%	44%	56%	46%
National		42%	59%	43%	35%	36%
No Preference		13%	11%	13%	9%	18%

Again, the higher social grades are more intent than the lower on financing the national stations when it comes to an exclusive choice. Given the small share of listening which BBC local radio attracts, and the enormous presence of the national networks, it is some measure of its strength that local radio commands such support from listeners for finite resources. It may, on a more flattering interpretation, simply reflect the extent of satisfaction with the national services: they fulfil their task so well that that no further funding is assumed to be needed.

British national radio has for many years now been structured on a 'streamed' basis; the content of each station has, by implication, directly contradicted the 'range and balance' provisions generally associated with public service broadcasting. Because listeners simply do not switch around, whether discouraged by the structure or as a consequence of the natural dynamics of listening behaviour, the central tenets of choice, range, education, information and entertainment, are meaningless unless regarded in the context of the whole system. Only at the local and regional levels have stations been expected to become public service microcosms, and a proliferation of local stations will relieve any individual stations of that burden – as long as the BBC remains to fulfil the role that the Green Paper has outlined for it and which the listening public most certainly endorses. The irony is in the reluctance with which many commercial station managers will surrender their role in the local community which has been equally founded on the application of public service principles to daily practices. While they currently, and with some justification, covet their standing within the community, many are also aware that the effects of competition might force them to abandon some of the community service principles which they have assiduously encouraged.

CHAPTER 11

Managing the Future: The Voice of the Industry

The extensive interviews which were undertaken with station managers and other senior figures in the radio industry allow for a comparison between their and the listeners' perspectives. For the sake of convenience and comprehensibility, this chapter is divided into four discrete sections which cover the most pressing issues raised during the interviews: Competition; Regulation; Copyright; and Public Service.

a) Competition

If one phrase could encapsulate attitudes of ILR managers to the prospects of existing ILR stations it is that, like the proverbial Irishman, they would not start from here. Many were unhappy that they had been asked, as they saw it, to play the game according to one set of rules which were about to be transformed radically after a great deal of energy and money had been expended. Competition in itself was not the problem; it was the disadvantaged nature of their position in comparison to new entrants. There were four different facets of this problem which concerned them.

First, those stations which rely on the cross-subsidisation inherent in the IBA system of rental charges are genuinely concerned about the uneconomic costs of owning or renting the necessary transmitters. This is certainly not surprising when one compares the £8000 p.a. paid by Moray Firth with the £350,000 p.a. for Radio Clyde. The larger stations agree; as one manager put it: "Some of the very small stations don't have a hope in hell of making it in the commercial world. If cross-subsidisation was taken away a lot of small stations would not exist."

This was echoed elsewhere: "I think smaller stations would disappear overnight because . . . national revenues will go down. I can see something like 60% to 70% of the existing stations going out of business very quickly indeed." One industry figure agreed that this would be the price for an unfettered existence: "You can't have all the opportunities and all the freedom for the operators, which is inherent in the Green Paper, without the risk attached." For one of the bigger stations in a position to benefit, the risk was also acknowledged with less alarm:

109

"We'll lose some of the protection, we're a protected species, but if that's traded off against opportunities that's OK with me."

Even those who are optimistic about the future are concerned about the transition from their current statutory requirements to the free market. One station which had been capitalised on the basis of two fully-equipped and expensive studios in order to meet IBA franchise requirements would never have become involved in such expenditure in a market-led system. It was worried about being saddled with an uneconomic (albeit very high quality) transmission system while new competitors under the new system remain unburdened. One very bullish MD was as concerned as everyone about the transition period: "The final solution is utterly compelling. The skill is getting from here to there with a certain amount of elegance."

A less pessimistic analysis suggested that small stations could survive by sacrificing a part of their transmission area. Poor reception was a risk, as the standards currently imposed by the IBA might be relaxed, but the real risk was that "the contractor would be forced by circumstances to reduce the size of the area it covers." These stations would not necessarily fail completely, but would simply reduce their coverage to the outlying areas which are uneconomic to reach.

The second area of concern was the ability of *genuinely* local stations to survive as profits decline, economies of scale become increasingly vital, and the larger predatory companies seek to take over the smaller ones. One manager who had responsibility for three stations was adamant about the invaluable cost savings in management, technical staff and capital equipment, and did not accept that the output was any less "local." The opposite view was described by a commercial MD who had observed several takeovers in the manoeuvres for survival and doubted whether the best local interests of one station could be served under the ownership of another with its roots in a completely different locality. These considerations are relevant to those stations which operate as an integral part of a locality, perhaps less so for those which choose an exclusively music formula. It is a dilemma which goes to the heart of the Green Paper's title: there may be more stations in the locality, but will there be more local stations? There may conceivably be less in the long run, as economies of scale force more mergers and takeovers and erode any unique feeling of local identity.

A logical extension of this concern was expressed by some ILR managers, aimed at investors from outside the country – in particular, Australia. It was especially galling for those who had suffered self-deprivation and struggled to build a successful business founded on a valued service to the local community, only to see "people from outside this country just walk in and buy a piece of the action. Instead of worrying about programming, I spent a lot more of my time worrying about the shareholders. There ought to be very strong restrictions on people who can buy into this country from outside the EEC." Local identity may, in other words, be difficult to generate from some distant part of the UK; it is downright impossible from Sydney.

The third area of concern was the imminent arrival of independent national radio. As the internal industry disagreements testify, there is no unanimity on the benefits or otherwise of INR. The advertisers, predictably, are adamant that nothing less than three new commercial channels which together are capable of reaching 80% or more of the total population will lift radio out of its lowly commercial status of "the 2% medium." Once advertisers perceive the reach, accessibility and relative cheapness of national commercial radio, they will begin to invest in it. Its status will rise amongst creative staff, and a more professional approach to radio advertisements will fuel its popularity. Other local or community-type stations may benefit but only as "fine-tuning"; the main thrust will come from the national stations.

It is well known that this position is supported by a few of the larger stations. According to one, INR, far from having a debilitating effect on existing stations, will attract additional audiences for everyone. More money will be generated by the availability of new audiences, and all radio will benefit as a result. It is the quality of the audience and its relevance to the major advertisers that matters, and a national radio audience could increase the total share of advertising available to all radio.

The majority of stations, however, are worried about INR – in the words of one, it is "only those who hope they'll be in it" who are unconcerned while the rest are engaged in a "damage limitation exercise" in order to mitigate the worst effects. It is their belief that local radio stations will be forced into the local marketplace for their revenue and that any national revenue should constitute an unexpected bonus. Thus, one medium-sized station anticipated very hard times for those stations which relied on national advertising for their survival: "Some of the big stations leave us standing at the national level but have not developed their local side; they are going to get a caning when the national channels start. They only have themselves to blame." He was damning in his criticism of local sales forces and believed that more energy expended would have prevented radio from becoming the advertising backwater which it currently is.

It was clear that regional factors were important in this advertising equation. One northern manager said he would be in trouble if he had to rely on local advertising alone against his current cost base: "The southern regions traditionally do badly on reach – about 50% less, but

111

my goodness look at their revenues. If we lost half our audience we'd be in real trouble. The prosperity of the region is important." Because local newspapers set the competitive rate, which is traditionally higher in the South, southern stations can afford to charge more for equivalent audience sizes and profiles than their northern counterparts. This imbalance highlights the social factors which work independently of radio itself and are a function of the regional infrastructure: it means that the "market" in some areas will support more (or better) radio than in others, irrespective of the needs or wants of the local population, because of the prosperity of the audience. Uniform legislation may not have a uniform effect.

The fourth area of concern was the effect of competition on programming. The philosophy of many ILR executives may best be summarised as a convenient convergence of commercial self-interest and commitment to the community. "Our local news is our strength", said one MD, and many emphasised the role and importance which ILR stations had attained within the local community. As we have seen, this represents more than idle boasting: many ILR stations have succeeded in attracting a loyal and appreciative audience.

The level of commitment to and involvement with the local community was, inevitably, tempered by the cost. Maintaining a reasonable contingent of journalistic staff often stretched resources, but was deemed essential to the news credibility of the station. The news service of those stations which had been forced to pare their news staff to the bone, were regarded with some scepticism, but may also represent what is to come after de-regulation; at some stage, the economics of news production inhibits the ability to provide a comprehensive service, even if listeners would prefer it: "We have news bulletins every hour on the hour – we would stop that and only have them at peak times, perhaps in the morning. All these things are reducing local choice, not enhancing it." *Increasing* the news content in order to establish a different identity from other suppliers, or even maintaining existing levels, were not viable options: "It wouldn't make economic sense. The theory of it's there, but you would be so financially weakened that . . . the sums just wouldn't add up to do more on a declining revenue."

In the competitive future, therefore, even though news and information constitutes "an integral part of our service and our appeal", there was considerable uncertainty about its survival. "We would have to reposition ourselves in the marketplace", said one, while another: "We would certainly continue to carry news of a kind; whether as comprehensive a service as we do now would be a consideration to be made at the time." One ILR manager had different views on what should constitute news output on a local station, and was therefore less

112

worried about the consequences: "When people talk about local news, they are really talking about gossip . . . they are not talking about huge political issues."

Other elements of non-music programming were clearly too expensive and inappropriate for commercial stations. Major outside broadcast operations were out of the question, as was drama. Several times, the original IBA drama obligations were roundly condemned as being totally unrealistic; plays on ILR could not be sustained by a free market and only IBA requirements had forced stations to attempt them. One of the more aggressive companies, which used to undertake plays and documentaries, said they were the first to go: "They were one of the first things we stopped doing when the IBA took their foot off the brake." The problem was illustrated by one station which now does about one play every two years. It required drama producer, back-up staff, Equity rates for actors, and other specially recruited freelance staff all of which amounted to "sheer self-indulgence" for small audiences. The one station which still employs a drama producer nearly axed the position two years ago: "Plays themselves are not popular and in terms of value for money in getting audiences they are undoubtedly a total waste of money."

While competition and de-regulation are aimed directly and exclusively at the commercial sector, and the BBC's role in local radio is explicitly identified in the Green Paper, the BBC does not operate in a vacuum. Fragmentation of audiences will inevitably reduce the audience base for BBC stations, as it will for others and will have repercussions for credibility if not immediate economic survival: "Audiences are important, and if we are to be a voice in the community, it seems to me that a significant proportion of the community has to be listening to us." It is axiomatic that whatever a station's source of revenue, its self-estimation and even its continued existence depends on maintaining an audience of sufficient size to warrant an operation: "Once the majority of people no longer use BBC services, they aren't going to want to pay for it. . . . I think that is a great danger." As money becomes tighter within the BBC itself, the exigencies of television production may erode the resources which successive managements are prepared to devote to a service of apparently declining usefulness. There are vulnerable groups whose value to advertisers is too minimal for commercial stations to embrace: one area which tended to attract a disproportionate number of retired people – described a little uncharitably as "God's waiting-room" – best highlights the dilemma for a local BBC station which would have extra responsibility for this sector but would at the same time be attempting to provide for other special groups. Balancing acts on declining audience bases will place BBC local stations in increasingly precarious positions.

b) Regulation

Independent Local Radio in its earlier days did, according to almost every MD we spoke to, suffer from the regulatory structure imposed by Government and interpreted by the IBA. Most were unwilling to lay too much blame directly at the feet of the IBA, whose job was to interpret someone else's message. According to one founding MD of a successful station: "The IBA have come out on the wrong side of this. They were stuck with a very difficult Act of Parliament and they have done their best with it. It has been the Act of Parliament that has been the problem, not the IBA." While the Act was certainly restrictive, the IBA according to another MD is not blameless: it "had a lot more flexibility than it displayed" even under existing legislation and could have shown greater sensitivity to and understanding of local radio.

Most were a good deal happier with the IBA under the new regime of the last 12–18 months when, as one put it, "the shackles have come off", and less programming demands have been made to ensure survival. For the immediate future, however, little change in programming is anticipated despite the relaxation of programming obligations. One MD maintained: "We would do what we are doing now even with light touch control. The IBA never bothered us." Another was similarly committed to existing policy: "I don't think the senior staff at this radio station are a million miles away from what the IBA would like to see." As we shall see, the BBC background of some commercial radio managers had instilled in them a commitment to the old tenets of public service broadcasting which they would like to maintain as long as their station could remain profitable.

For the future, there was a general appreciation that a lighter touch is desirable, but some disagreement as to whether any new body was necessary. The IBA had some support, although by no means uncritical. One critic felt that the IBA had a credibility problem despite its track record and some excellent staff. In the light of past experience, there was no guarantee, he said, that the lighter touch would remain so once profitability was attained and things were going well. His preference was for a new Regulatory Authority. Another manager, however, was adamant that the IBA was the only realistic option and that it really could not be blamed for the unreasonable onus imposed on it by repressive Government legislation.

A further point made in support of the IBA was its impressive record on provision of technical services. As one manager said: "Laser was off the air every week – we pay a lot to the IBA but we get a Rolls Royce service." The importance of continuous transmission for revenue was important: "One of the strengths of this system is that we have never had to say to an advertiser we have lost your commercial because we lost

114

the output. Because it has never happened, people do not realise the dangers."

One of the frequent criticisms of the IBA was the perception that radio was only ever treated as "television without pictures", and regulated accordingly without any feel for its special status. It is this perception which has led to expressions of sympathy for a completely new authority which would devote itself entirely to the administration of a new regulatory regime unencumbered by any reference to regulatory frameworks applicable to other media. The Canadian model was suggested by one manager as a good half-way house: anyone who can provide evidence of a technical and audience gap in the market is allocated a frequency. This was described as a "means of ensuring diversity" because applicants were generally required to prove complementarity. The licence granted was transferable but very specific, even down to programme formatting; any unauthorised variation resulted in revocation of the licence.

Regulation should be applied without fear or favour across the board, with no special exemptions for particular groups, although one MD thought that existing stations would be handicapped by predating new legislation: "If you're going to have a whole rack of commercial radio stations, then we've got to be allowed to compete on exactly the same terms. But we won't be because . . . the capital investment's gone into it." Even those most excited by the prospect of de-regulation did not want the explosion of the American model: "I think you would lose something if you took all the regulations away but nothing like as much as the critics fear." One manager perhaps summed up the general feeling: "The debate should not be about the authority but the regulations. What is needed is a proper framework; the idea of a free-for-all would be chaos."

c) **Copyright**

If any one single issue can be guaranteed to provoke acute apoplexy in any ILR Manager, it is the problem of copyright. In every interview, without exception, this issue was raised as perhaps the most trenchant obstacle to reform and expansion in the commercial radio sector. "Copyright has to be sorted out; it is a scandal," was the universal view echoed in many different ways.

Of the two main copyright bodies, most managers were prepared to differentiate philosophically between the Performing Rights Society and Phonographic Performance Ltd. Payments to PRS were more acceptable because artists and composers had a rightful claim to be rewarded for their creativity and originality. Although no ILR stations welcomed the prospect of additional expenditure, PRS royalties were not generally held to be unreasonable or excessive. PPL, on the other hand, were portrayed as a grasping and greedy monopoly enterprise hiding behind the privilege conferred by the 1956 Copyright Act. The sliding scale of proportional payments which ILR stations are bound to make are regarded as a major contribution to the parlous financial state that many of the stations have found themselves in. One station, whose total annual copyright bill came to £250,000, was concerned about the debilitating effect such expenditure would have on news output: "You can employ an awful lot of journalists on a quarter of a million, even at NUJ rates."

Insult is added to injury by the numbers of record "pluggers" which, it was constantly being claimed, were touring the independent stations in (usually) vain attempts to persuade DJs to play the discs of one record label rather than another. Instead of the stations paying PPL, they unanimously claimed, the positions should be reversed. The root cause of the problem, said one MD, was the ILR monopoly which itself bred the music publishers' monopoly – with the result that the two had become "locked in a death embrace." The only possible reform was a change in the legislation.

The bad feeling towards PPL was exacerbated by the needle-time limitations. It was originally believed that no further time was negotiable because of a PPL agreement with the Musicians' Union, but subsequent discussions have shown more needle-time available – for the right money. This was less contentious among the existing stations, some of whom would not necessarily use more than nine hours a day, but could become prohibitively expensive for 24-hour music stations which would require the additional programming. This restriction was seen as the major obstacle to any progress towards genuine single strand or "community of interest" programming: a jazz or country music station could not provide a proper service unless it was a 24-hour station; that, in turn, would require a very special (and so far non-existent) deal with PPL.

PPL, for their part, are concerned that their position has been increasingly distorted. The *average* payment per disc, they claim, is 77p over the 47 stations; while the more successful stations at the peak of their earnings will certainly pay substantially more, that is a fair distribution for using the product of the commercial record companies.

Their argument is based on the premise that the ILR stations should pay a commercial rate for a product which is commercially useful to them. Given that PPL music represents some 60% of programming output (and arguably a much larger proportion of advertising revenue), it argues that 4–7% of Net Advertising Revenue does not represent an

116

unreasonable demand. Because it is set as a proportion of revenue, PPL did no more than share in the success of any station using its product – a failed or ailing station meant little or no revenue.

The needle-time limit had its origins in a deal struck with the IBA when nine hours emerged as a compromise between the need for recorded music and the Musicians' Union concerns over reduced opportunities for live music. Although PPL, due to its own reliance on musicians, could never unilaterally accept huge increases in needle-time, it believed the MU is now more pragmatic and therefore prepared to accede to demands. Hence the new flexibility.

The two major justifications for the PPL position were quoted as originating in the long-running case referred by the Association of Independent Radio Contractors (AIRC) to the Performing Right Tribunal. The PRT were quoted as saying that they were satisfied with the evidence of the "value of our records to the radio stations"; furthermore, they were satisfied with the evidence showing no proof of increased record sales as a result of radio airplay. In fact, even one of the ILR managers conceded that "record sales have fallen quite dramatically" and that secondary income must therefore become more important. If the PPL analysis is true, that there is evidence of more and more usage but less and less purchase, their determination to maintain the current position becomes more understandable.

It is an area fraught with difficulty, and station managers were unanimous in their conviction that a relaxation of the copyright rules were an essential precondition to the healthy expansion of music radio. The very survival of some stations against a national network might depend on lifting this burden: "If you can reduce the cost of copyright charges, you can bring in a national service and that would be OK."

d) Public service

To date, the concept of public service – however it may be defined – has been applied to both BBC and ILR, the former through an extension of its Charter obligations and corporate philosophy, the latter through the various Broadcasting Acts as interpreted and administered by the IBA. This final section examines the current attitudes towards this concept amongst practitioners in the private and public sectors.

Many ILR managers are themselves imbued with the BBC tradition and identify a responsibility beyond delivering mass audiences to advertisers. They believe in extending other public service principles, apart from impartiality in news and current affairs, to the private sector. Said one: "It's not just a business, it's very much a social responsibility running a radio station; it is a responsibility to broadcast to the whole community rather than just part of it." These managers believe in the public service tradition with sufficient fervour to embrace it even without the constraining legislation; they have aspirations beyond the accumulation of large profits through wall-to-wall pop broadcasting.

Their vision of the "successful" local commercial station sees it as a focus for the community which reflects and enhances local spirit, and fulfils local needs for news, information, advice and assistance. They believe it to be of genuine benefit to the local community. At the moment this ideological commitment is rewarded financially as well as philosophically. As stations have struggled to survive, they have been progressively released by the IBA from their franchise commitments to drama, educational programmes, a full complement of news staff and sponsorship restrictions. The one remaining public service role – their claim to identify with and represent the community – is seen as integral for their continued success. The question arises: is this commitment likely to continue if it no longer contributes to a station's profitability? Many fear that as stations proliferate and audiences fragment, far from consolidating their local identity, stations will be forced into single-strand specialist programming in order to protect their profitability against a falling revenue base.

Some BBC managers are in no doubt as to the direction in which ILR will have to go. One with first-hand experience of ILR compared the priorities under the systems. In commercial radio, he said, there is only one maxim which dictates all programming decisions: "The bottom line at the end of the year." He acknowledged the public service aspirations of many ILR managers, but quoted the experience of at least one ILR station to demonstrate how expensive news programming will be drastically cut if revenue runs short.

The essence of the BBC position is that all communities have news and information needs which deserve to be fulfilled, and that all sectors of each community have some right to recognition. Their presence should be guaranteed and not be contingent either on the relative competence of a marketing and sales department or on the market value of an audience. The information and advice needs of pensioners or the unemployed or low-earning ethnic groups – all of limited value to advertisers – are probably greater than most; as licence-fee payers they have every right to expect an equal and adequate service to meet their needs. "I know from the letters and comments I get that we are a friend to the inadequate and the lonely, but also to the normal individual out there who just wants to know what's going on around them."

This applies to any of the separate regions, although some are felt to have a more definable local identity than others. In areas which may be

118

considered less socially cohesive – the Home Counties, for example, compared to Humberside or Merseyside – there is still a community feeling which deserves its own service: "It is right for people living in Bedfordshire to have their station." Areas like Bedfordshire, Sussex and Kent "have strong local identities and their own problems and cultures; they have every right where possible to have those cultures expressed and identity re-enforced even if it is closer to the Capital."

It was not just the local communities but the national news service that would suffer from an impoverished BBC local radio: "If you listen to Radio 4 you'll hear living evidence of the majority of the country's non-metropolitan news reported by local radio, which is an enormously valuable resource." Both in terms of the daily input to national news and information and as a training ground for tomorrow's top reporters, local radio serves the country: "Michael Buerk, Kate Adey, John Motson are all people who have come up through local radio."

The concern of one manager was that the BBC would eventually pull out of local radio, leaving no community equivalent; for this reason, he felt, involvement should not be left to the BBC's discretion but for the sake of all listeners should be an obligation explicitly imposed upon them. Those programmes which rely on speech are often designed to fulfil community education or information requirements which would simply not fit the commercial style, especially in an environment of increased competition: debates with local councillors, information on how the councillors are elected, how the rates are set etc. have all featured in BBC output and been appreciated within the local community. On one interpretation, this kind of input is a genuine contribution to democracy because citizens can question their representatives and because local radio stations by their nature are less susceptible to manipulation. Local radio can therefore contribute to the essential democratic process as well as providing a forum for local information and entertainment.

Maintaining appeal to many different minorities is an intrinsic element of the BBC philosophy, while at the same time ensuring an audience share and reach which can justify the station's existence: "We are about the community" said one, but all constituent parts of that community. "If running radio is about mass appeal", said another "then I'm going to scrap my ethnic programmes tomorrow; if it's about mass appeal, you won't be doing education or religious programmes. Surely it is about relating to a community – there are lots and lots of minority groups who look to the BBC and their local station to provide them with the sort of information they need. This is why we will do programmes for the disabled and visually handicapped, cover local history and minority sports. You won't get any of those programmes within hearing distance of this town." Even the introduction of dedicated ethnic stations would not obviate the need for programmes devoted to the same minorities, because within any genre of music or speech there are infinite variations and preferences: it is as easy for subgroups of minorities to be unprovided for as it is for whole minorities.

Perhaps the essence of BBC presence in local radio is the treatment of the listener as citizen rather than consumer. One manager expounded his theory that the significance of the BBC station increases in direct proportion to the listener's responsibilities: as the teenager becomes a ratepayer with roots in the community, affected by the local decisions, the local economy and business life, so he or she will seek the requisite daily-life information from the local media; local radio is the most up to date and most easily accessible. While ILR provides some of these needs for some of the people, it cannot afford to satisfy minorities, whether they be differentiated on grounds of age, ethnic origin, music taste or sporting preference. Commercial radio, even when operating as a monopoly, can only aspire to serving the community as long as the community is of value to advertisers; its continued execution of this role under increased competitive pressure can hardly be guaranteed.

CHAPTER 12

Summary and Conclusions –
Any Answers?

12.1 The media environment

It is arguably an unfortunate accident of timing that radio is set to undergo an unprecedented expansion at the very moment that satellite technology is due to double the number of available television channels. It is a coincidence of technological opportunity that large sectors of the population will be facing such unparalleled competition for their viewing and listening time.

At a time when new radio services will be trying to entice listeners out of some fairly entrenched listening habits, the prospect of a surge of competition from the more dominant medium will not be welcomed. While the volume of listening and viewing may increase to some extent, there is no possibility of it matching the exponential growth rate of new media. Audiences will fragment, and will inevitably diminish for *all* services, with serious commercial implications for the total media environment.

For commercial radio in particular, whose recent past and present has looked healthy and profitable, the proliferation of media opportunities will have repercussions. The recent upsurge in advertising revenue for ILR is rooted partly in the perceived high cost of television air-time: some national advertisers who are not convinced that these costs represent a sensible return on investment in advertising are turning to network advertising on radio, at vastly cheaper rates, to supplant rather than supplement traditional TV campaign expenditure. Since advertisers had been prepared to invest in a medium which is known to reach less than half of the population, there has been plenty of optimism about genuinely national commercial services which could increase the audience for commercial stations to over 80% of the population.

The additional commercial TV air-time is likely to be unsettling for two reasons. First, the introduction of competition for terrestrial commercial television may itself drive down advertising rates; advertisers who have disqualified themselves from television on cost grounds will therefore reconsider, and may return to the more powerful medium at the expense of national radio. Secondly, there would be a good deal more peripheral TV air-time – to smaller audiences but at proportionately lower cost – for smaller advertisers who find the current television rates too excessive. It is precisely these new players in the advertising game for whom national commercial radio may be ideal; in the not too distant future, they will be faced with awkward decisions and some, again, will surely be unable to resist the temptations of a cheap spot on television.

This is the setting in which the new policies on radio will be implemented. The structure of radio will undergo a dramatic and explosive change which will not only provide a host of new listening opportunities, but will also – given the projected fragmentation of audiences – have implications for the existing radio services. The regulatory structure which the Government constructs, or the criteria which the new Radio Authority is directed to adopt in the selection of successful applicants, will fashion the character, quality and range of new listening opportunities. This study has offered some insight into what sort of choices and opportunities listeners want; what follows is a summary of the key findings.

12.2 Attitudes to existing radio services

Satisfaction levels with existing stations are high; there are few complaints with the range of programmes available, and the national services in particular are generally held in very high regard. Appreciation for the quality of these stations and for the service as a whole is very high indeed, while television is held in comparatively low esteem: only 4% expressed any dissatisfaction with radio programmes compared to 37% for television programmes. As a consequence, there is some perplexity about the need for more radio services at all; more television would be welcomed with somewhat greater alacrity.

A more detailed examination of these generalised findings reveals a demand for a wider range of radio services as long as the current range is left intact. Listening habits are more entrenched than viewing: over the course of a week, more than four out of five listeners will listen to no more than two radio stations. There is therefore greater conservatism and the objects of affection are jealously guarded. If the addition of new services is perceived as having a materially detrimental effect on the high quality associated with the existing service, the majority of the audience would be distinctly displeased. If, on the other hand, the new services can achieve the right balance of variety and quality without endangering the existing ecology, most listeners would like to hear more of certain categories of speech and music programmes.

12.3 The demand for more

No categorisation of programme types can be exhaustive, but there was clear evidence of demand for certain types of music and speech programming. In an attempt to embrace the spectrum of musical taste, eleven types of music were identified. At the older end of the age spectrum, there was support for more Big Band music from 46% of those who enjoyed that type of music; at the younger end, 44% of contemporary specialist music fans wanted more of such music. More Country and Western music was favoured by 45% across most ages, and more Jazz by 41%. These were the preferences of larger minorities rather than overwhelming majorities: clues to what new services may profitably include rather than definitive blueprints. For all music categories, most listeners with an appetite for more found the prospect of new stations incorporating such music very appealing.

The categorisation of speech-based programming encompassed twenty different genres, and demand was slightly lower overall than for music categories. Certain categories were again more prominent than others: more radio plays were supported by 36% of those who currently listen to plays, more comedy programmes by 35%, more short stories 33%, more documentaries and more sports programmes each by 32%. Again, most of these listeners found the prospect of new stations which featured their favourite types of programme very appealing.

12.4 Catering for ethnic minorities

While studies of this kind include by definition a series of generalisations about the total audience, there are certain sectors of this audience for whom these generalisations are less applicable. This research elected to devote particular attention to two ethnic groups, Asians and Afro-Caribbeans; both expressed considerable frustration at the lack of any appropriate radio dedicated to their particular ethnic and cultural requirements. Similar conclusions would almost certainly apply to the many other groups of different cultural and ethnic backgrounds, and there can be no doubt of the strength of demand for ethnic music and ethnic speech programmes – both in English and original languages – aimed specifically at ethnic communities both locally and nationally.

The survey of Afro-Caribbeans confirmed, in particular, the demand for specialist music stations to which numerous pirate stations already attest. Nearly half of this group said they listened to pirate stations, and were as enthusiastic about the nature and style of presentation as about the music content. The survey of Asians demonstrated a different emphasis, with 58% favouring Asian language programmes and 56%

English language programmes aimed at Asians. Amongst both groups, there was a keen awareness that the existence of such programmes, available as much to interested non-ethnics as to the ethnic communities themselves, could be of valuable service in promoting the understanding and appreciation of minority cultures.

12.5 Attitudes to commercial radio

Expansion of the radio sector is contingent not only on advertisers' attraction to the medium, but crucially on the willingness of radio listeners to accept some form of commercialism as an intrinsic element of their listening experience. The prospect of programmes being offered within a commercial environment tends to temper, but not extinguish, the enthusiasm of those who want new stations which schedule more of their favourite programme types. For both music and speech programmes, sponsorship as a means of earning commercial revenue was more tolerable than spot advertising. For some speech programmes (plays, in particular), commercial breaks within programmes would prove an outright deterrent for a small minority of listeners, although most claimed they would be less likely to listen. Given the relative cost of speech-based radio production, and the evidence of demand for more of the Radio 4 type of output, the lower resistance to sponsorship suggests that it might prove the more acceptable short-term route for attracting audiences who could be easily alienated from an over-commercialised station.

Perhaps unsurprisingly in a country with no more than fifteen years experience of commercial radio, there is considerable opposition to the form which it takes. Even amongst regular listeners to independent radio, the commercials are frequently regarded as repetitive, intrusive, creatively barren and not infrequently a positive obstacle to enjoying the accompanying programme. One-fifth of the population have never heard any commercial radio, and more than a quarter claim to have tried and then deserted it; whether the reasons for this reluctance are contentment with non-commercial stations or the unpleasant connotations of radio with advertisements, it will need a sensitive and subtle induction policy with the right programming mix to entice an unwilling sector of the audience into an unfamiliar fold.

12.6 Attitudes to local and neighbourhood radio

Assessing demand for non-existent services is problematic, especially when compounded by the definitional problem of what constitutes 'local' radio. Overall, the emerging pattern appears to suggest some support for local stations covering similar areas to the existing ILR stations, but more limited support for smaller local stations: 42% expressed interest in a neighbourhood station covering their town or a wider area, and the same proportion were not interested in any kind of neighbourhood radio; 10% expressed support for a station limited to a part of the town or a five-mile radius. Apart from London, which clearly lacked any sense of unified identity, it was the nearest town or city which constituted the focus of concern for most listeners as the centre of their activity and information needs. The prospect of more localised neighbourhood stations therefore did not excite many listeners, because they could not envisage how the programme content of such stations could prove enticing.

There was some enthusiasm for active participation in local radio: 18% of those who wanted new neighbourhood stations expressed an interest in running them and 33% in helping to make occasional programmes. While such stations are unlikely to attract more than a small minority either to listen or participate in them, support in some local areas will be more forthcoming than others; it is impossible for a survey of this size to identify small pockets of individuals who would be particularly likely to appreciate the benefits.

The two exceptions to this general evidence are ethnic groups and the London area. It was abundantly clear that dedicated ethnic stations had enthusiastic backing amongst both the Asian and Afro-Caribbean community: 66% of the former and 75% of the latter supported local stations directed at their own communities. The two groups were divided, however, on participation. While the proportion of Asians prepared to volunteer their active participation in a local ethnic station was similar to the national sample, enthusiasm was demonstrably higher amongst Afro-Caribbeans: 41% said they would like to be involved in running the station and 51% in making occasional programmes. While it was not feasible to extend the number of ethnic groups under consideration, it would be reasonable to generalise these findings to other groups of different cultural and ethnic background.

Within the Capital, there were some indications that neighbourhood stations would serve as a valuable means of mitigating the worst effects of the big city with no obvious focus for attachment. The sheer size of the population and geographical area, the kaleidoscope of different cultures and languages, and the contrasting characters of even neighbouring areas in London, all suggest that a different approach to serving this sector of the population will be required. Small stations serving not only different cultural needs, but different age groups and discrete musical tastes would be welcomed and in some cases help to alleviate some of the isolation of the big city. It is possible that other

125

metropolitan areas may benefit, but none have the same sprawling heterogeneity which arguably deserves special treatment.

Reactions to existing local radio output suggest that concerns about amateurism will constitue the major barrier to success for local stations: over half of listeners felt that commercial local radio was less professional than BBC national radio. Even some of local radio's most ardent supporters, both BBC and commercial, were prone to complain about a less professional output in music presentation (with the noted exception of the Afro-Caribbean listeners). While the strength of these stations undoubtedly lay in their immersion in the local area and their ability to represent and reflect local character and problems, listeners were impatient with standards which fell below the established BBC practice. The BBC still represents the dominant yardstick for quality, and the programme formats and content of new local stations will have to strike the right listening chord or create new listening models to compensate for a perceived inferiority in the standards of presentation.

12.7 Radio and Public Service

The public service obligations which have traditionally informed British broadcasting are as significant for radio as they are for television. Whatever the liberating implications of de-regulation, there are certain tenets of public service which remain sufficiently embedded in the public consciousness to warrant serious consideration. Stations which cater to minority tastes, such as Radio 3, are established for most listeners as an invaluable part of the radio landscape – amongst those who never use it as much as its serious followers. Three-quarters of listeners approve of the requirement for news reporting on all stations, but half would prefer less frequent breaks; balance and impartiality in news reporting has almost unanimous approval.

Stations are not expected to be microcosms of the public service ethos, each covering a range of programmes and an appropriate balance of education, information and entertainment. The system as a whole, however, is perceived currently as providing an adequate range, which listeners want to see maintained. The role of the BBC in providing a network of local stations is generally supported. It is difficult to define any concept of quality in radio broadcasting, let alone quantify attitudes towards it; most listeners, however, believe that the current system – and the national services in particular – embodies the quality of radio service to which other services should aspire. Any interference with the current system which might be responsible for a deterioration in quality would be too great a sacrifice for an increased aggregate of stations.

12.8 Conclusions

It is neither unreasonable nor untypical of the human condition to prefer the status quo to the uncertainty of change. When the status quo actually represents, if not an ideal state, a state from which the majority derive considerable enjoyment, any alteration needs to be undertaken with care. There are, most certainly, unmet needs for which the newly-available spectrum should be harnessed. There are also sacred cows, such as local news and information, minority taste broadcasting and range of programmes, which need to be preserved. Above all, there is recognition of an innate quality in British radio, a degree of professionalism and commitment which could be diminished or distilled amidst the proliferation of new stations. The commitment to quality has priority over any promises of greater quantity.

It will be a delicate and sensitive balancing act indeed which succeeds in increasing the number of stations within a framework of range and balance without upsetting the current stability of the radio ecology. In order to make a genuine contribution to widening the scope of available radio choice, the new national commercial stations will need to find creative as well as profitable solutions: resistance to commercials is high, not least because of the traditional dominance of non-commercial national radio and the relative youthfulness of commercial radio. Local radio will face the additional pressures of intense competition with local papers and freesheets. It will require patience while local advertisers, unfamiliar with the potential of this new market for promoting their own goods and services, are slowly educated into its advantages over the local media.

Because radio stations tend to command loyalty, audiences must be seduced out of well-established and entrenched listening habits. This research suggests that new stations which can create some genuinely original, imaginative and different listening opportunities should have a bright future. Initial progress will be slow, and considerable investment may be required to build audiences. The pressure to abandon franchise obligations in pursuit of a mass audience, which would result in the very convergence of programming which both Government and audience vigorously oppose, will intensify for both the new contractors and the new Radio Authority. Experience from other countries has demonstrated the dilemmas imposed on equivalent regulatory bodies or tribunals in similar situations. On the one hand they are mandated to impose sanctions on miscreants, which would jeopardise both jobs and the considerable capital investment; on the other hand, a more lenient interpretation could have considerable consequences for range and quality as struggling commercial stations are forced to push back the boundaries of their original strictly-defined terms of reference. The role

127

of the Radio Authority will be instrumental in maintaining the range and quality of the radio service.

At both national and local level, the demand for more and different radio exists, as long as a firm regulatory hand is prepared to redirect the deviant stations to the terms of their licence, and implement threats of confiscation. There is considerable scope for expansion in radio which could provide listeners with the enhanced opportunities which both they and the Government would like. To adapt the very apposite words of one independent station MD, the ultimate objective is utterly compelling; the skill is getting from here to there not only with elegance but leaving the range and quality of existing services intact.

Endpiece

This report has been founded entirely on the empirical evidence established through interviews with 40 industry figures, discussions with over 250 listeners around the country, and a representative survey of the population. Conclusions and interpretations have been drawn directly from the data and have avoided any preconceptions or expressions of opinion which could not be justified by the evidence. During the course of a year's immersion in such a complex field, however, it is inevitable that some judgements on the policy implications will be formed which do not emerge directly from the collected evidence. Two ideas in particular are presented here as our contribution to the continuing debate on how a de-regulated radio service might be most effectively organised.

The first stems from the local radio demands of listeners. It represents a structural suggestion in the use of one of the national medium wave frequencies, to assist in providing a more varied and stimulating commercial service to a great variety of different audiences. The second is a comment, in the light of this study, on the policy already propounded by the Government of auctioning the national commercial services.

1 Proposal for one national commercial station

At the end of Chapter 6, we alluded to the regulatory dilemma posed for the Regulatory Authority in those areas where different local audiences will be making conflicting but equally valid claims on available local frequencies. A successful franchise application for one audience sector must involve some deprivation for another. At the same time there will be individuals throughout the country with particular minority tastes, or with their roots in particular minority cultures, whose listening needs will not be served by any local stations. We believe that the development of an appropriate structural measure in national radio might serve to ameliorate both problems.

In principle, one of the national networks, possibly the current Radio 3 medium wave, could be made available to minority groups and operate on a Channel 4 commissioning basis. A network run on this basis would provide not only programmes for all cultural minorities,

129

but could include programmes for specialist interests as well: jazz music, popular classical, plays, documentaries, experimental comedy and a host of diverse programming strands serving many different minorities throughout the country. Stations which won a local franchise, but which could not afford much experimentation or speech-based programming, could dip into this station at any appropriate time; or switch to a night-time sustaining service at close-down; or tape and re-transmit at a time suitable for its own audience (e.g. ethnic shows broadcast late at night could be transmitted locally at any time considered most appropriate for the local ethnic audience). In short, the commitment to programming would have Channel 4 as its model; the operational arrangements would owe more to the current relationship between BBC local radio and Radio 2.

The concept is new in radio broadcasting, although variations have been proposed in other submissions to the Home Office. Its attraction would lie not only in its service to diverse communities but in its self-financing nature: for it is likely to prove especially appealing to advertisers. It would allow precision targetting of national minority audiences at a fraction of the cost of television audiences and almost certainly lower than the costs of air-time on the other two radio channels. In addition, revenue could be generated from user stations on a prescribed basis to supplement the station's income. It could be a perfect example of additional resources being harnessed to complement existing services and provide a genuine addition to consumer choice. The existence of such a service to the national population could then be included as one factor in the complicated equations which the Radio Authority will be required to resolve: all communities, even if they fail in securing a local frequency, will have some air-time to themselves, and listeners will not be completely disadvantaged by devotion to a minority interest or a decision to isolate themselves geographically from an ethnic community whose cultural tastes they share and appreciate. Just as Channel 4 has been hailed as another example of the British imagination and genius for encouraging a genuinely wide range of programmes and choice for television viewers, "Independent Radio Seven" could do the same for radio listeners.

2 Auctioning the national franchises

The proposed de-regulation of radio broadcasting will introduce a new element into the structure of British broadcasting with potentially profound and unpredictable implications: for the first time in this country, broadcasters will be allowed to *own* the means of transmission. While certain minimum technical standards are likely to be prescribed by the Radio Authority, studio facilities, sound equipment quality, and standards of transmission will be left to the successful franchise applicants. The establishment of a national network will require considerable capital investment. Even the most potentially profitable stations will, as we have seen, face a difficult struggle to win over audiences; this capital investment will constitute a substantial liability, and the temptation to deviate from the original franchise obligations in order to boost revenue will in some cases be immense. On the other hand, as suggested in the conclusions, a genuine range of services at both local and national level will depend on the Authority's determination to resist any such relaxation.

Under these circumstances, it is difficult to see how the auctioning of national franchises, exacerbating the financial burden on the successful operator and thereby reinforcing pressure on the Authority to exercise some latitude, can contribute to the creation of a better radio system offering genuine range and choice. While the medium and long term prospects of the new national stations are exciting, deep pockets will be required in the short term for capitalisation and to subsidise the initial losses. It will take time to attract audiences, build up loyalty and convince advertisers of the new commercial opportunities available to them. For those contemplating an application, the prospect of an auction may well deter potentially successful and innovative enterprises with limited investment resources; for successful candidates, the additional financial burden will reduce the margin of flexibility required to maintain a range and quality of programmes for initially small audiences. If we are concerned about the contribution which radio can make to both national entertainment and national culture, it is surely preferable that all available resources should be directed to producing better programmes rather than adding a barely discernible drop to the Treasury ocean.

APPENDIX I

Stage I: Interviewees in the Radio Industry

ILR Stations
Managing Director, Devon Air
Managing Director, Piccadilly
Managing Director, Capital
Managing Director, Invicta
Managing Director, Red Rose
Managing Director, Radio Clyde
Managing Director, Radio Trent
Managing Director, Broadland
Managing Director, Chiltern Radio
Managing Director, Radio City
Managing Director, Metro Radio

BBC Local Stations
Manager, Radio Devon
Manager, Radio London
Manager, Radio Manchester
Manager, Radio Kent
Manager, Radio Nottingham
Manager, Radio Norfolk
Manager, Radio Merseyside
Manager, Radio Cleveland
Manager, Radio Sussex
Manager, Radio Newcastle
Chief Asst., Radio Scotland

Advertisers
Leo Burnett
Young and Rubicam
TMD Advertising

Copyright Bodies
PPL
PRS
MCPS

Unions
Musicians Union
NUJ

Other Organisations
Cable Authority
Community Radio Association
AIRC
National Consumer Council

BBC Management
MD Radio
Deputy MD Radio

132

Controller of Local Radio
Head of Copyright

IBA
Director of Programmes, Radio
Senior Radio Research Officer

Stage II: Research Design for Group Discussions

For the qualitative stage, discussion groups were recruited according to five crucial variables: age, sex, social grade, region, and weight of listening, with additional groups to cater for youngsters and ethnic groups. Three of the variables were covered according to the following grid matrix:

	ABC1		C2DE	
	Older	Younger	Older	Younger
North	X			X
South		X	X	
Midlands	X			X
Wales		X	X	
Scotland	X			X
London		X	X	

This pattern was used for heavy radio listeners, with its mirror image (i.e., young ABC1 North etc.) applied to light listeners. In addition, there were two groups of Asians, one each in Southampton and Leeds; two groups of Afro-Caribbeans, one each in Wolverhampton and London; and two groups of teenagers, one each in Preston and Southampton. Half the groups consisted of men, half of women.

Stage III: Research Design for Survey

1. THE SAMPLE

1.1 The Main Sample

The main survey was conducted using a probability sample representative of the whole of Great Britain apart from the Outer Isles of Scotland. The sample was spread over 90 constituencies, which were chosen by selecting every other constituency from the NOP's standard 180 constituencies, used for the regular Random Omnibus Survey. This parent sample is drawn in the following way.

All GB constituencies, except for Orkney and Shetland and Western Isles, are first stratified by Registrar General's Standard Region. Within region they are further stratified by urban/rural mix, the four cells being Metropolitan (within the old Metropolitan Counties), Urban, Urban/Rural, and Rural, the difference between the last two being simply population density. This creates 46 cells in all (not all regions have all urban types), and within each cell constituencies are ranked according to the proportion of their population which falls within the professional or managerial classes. The population of each constituency is listed and cumulated, and 180 constituencies selected by applying a constant sampling interval to a random start point. In this way constituencies are selected with a probability proportional to size.

Within each constituency, a ward and then a polling district were selected at random. From a random start point an interval of 15 was repeatedly applied until 17 names had been selected (19 in ex-GLC constituencies). Individual electors were selected for interview, and no substitutes were taken.

There was also a process to ensure adults who were not on the Electoral Register had a chance of selection. At any address which contained any person aged 15 or over who was not on the Electoral Register – whether they be in addition to or instead of the selected elector – a further selection was undertaken using a Kish grid to choose one of the non-electors for interview. Thus in some cases two interviews could be conducted at the same address.

1.2 The Booster Samples

In addition to the main survey a series of booster interviews were conducted with different groups of particular interest, and these were all conducted using quota samples.

1.2.1 *The Asian Booster*

Nineteen areas were chosen which had a particularly high proportion of people from the Indian sub-continent. A target was set of four interviews in each area and quotas were set for age and sex.

1.2.2   The West Indian/African Booster
This was conducted in exactly the same way as the Asian Booster.

1.2.3   The Teenage Booster
The teenage booster covered only people aged 15 and 16. Quotas were set for sex and social class, and 13 constituencies were used for this booster.

1.2.4   The Rural Booster
This sample was different from the other boosters in that it was based on the ACORN classification of residential areas. Three ACORN types were identified as of particular interest to the survey:
   a)   Group A   Agricultural Areas
   b)   Type C10 Villages with non-farm employment
   c)   Type J35   Villages with wealthy older commuters
CACI drew a sample of 16 enumeration districts from all those enumerative districts across the whole country which fall into the three ACORN types. The 16 were split into 8 Group A, 5 Type C10 and 3 Type J35. Quotas were set for sex interlocked with working status, and age.

2.   THE QUESTIONNAIRE

A first draft of the questionnaire was tested in a pilot study, conducted at the beginning of October. Four interviewers conducted a total of 23 interviews, followed by full debriefing sessions.

As a result of the pilot the questionnaire was modified and shortened to bring the interview length down to target level. A final version was then drawn up, but after printing the Home Office requested some extra questions. These were sent to the interviewers in the form of a separate sheet to be added to all questionnaires, and these additional questions were asked on all but 33 interviews.

After fieldwork on the main stage had been completed, questionnaires were drawn up for the four boosters. These consisted of a common core of questions from the main questionnaire, with a number of questions deleted and replaced by questions of direct relevance to the target group.

3.   FIELDWORK

Interviewing took place on the main sample between October 16 and November 8 1987, and 90 interviewers worked on the survey. From the 1550 names issued on the survey 997 interviews were completed. Allowing for non-residential addresses, and electors who had moved or died, but including all the non-electors located on the survey, this represents a contact rate of 65%. The calculation of the contact rate is shown on the next page.

Elector Sample

Names Issued	1550
Non-residential	26
Elector died/moved	242
Effective sample	1282
Elector interviews	881
Elector contact rate	69%

Non-Elector Sample

Non-electors located	260
Non-elector interviews	116
Non-elector sample	45%

Total Sample

Effective sample	1542
Interviews	997
Contact Rate	65%

The Asian booster was conducted by 19 interviewers between November 27 and 29, and 71 interviews were conducted. The West Indian/African booster was conducted by 19 interviewers over the same dates, and 73 interviews were conducted.

Thirteen interviewers conducted 49 interviews on the teenage booster between November 27 and December 2, and 16 interviewers conducted 129 interviews on the rual booster between December 10 and 13.

4 ANALYSIS

The questionnaire contained several open-ended questions, and for each of these code frames were drawn up from listings of the first 100 replies. The code frames were agreed with the BRU before coding began. Once the coding was complete the data were transferred to NOP's in house computer. All data entry was subject to 100% verification. The data were subjected to a full computer edit to check for missing data, redundancy, and logical inconsistencies.

At this stage the profile of the sample was checked against best estimates for the population as a whole, to see if there were any discrepancies which needed to be corrected by weighting. Although there were some differences it was felt that it would be better not to weight the data, given the increase in survey error which weighting itself causes.

The final stage of the analysis was production of some 1000 computer tables, to a specification supplied by the BRU. The tables included analysis by one derived variable – "Radio Listening", broken into heavy, medium and light.

This was calculated by using the detailed information on how long the radio is listened to at different periods to produce for each respondent a figure for the total number of hours listened to in a week. The three analysis cells were formed by dividing the resulting values into the three terciles.

Broadcasting Research Unit Publications

The Public Service Idea in British Broadcasting: Main Principles
BRU (1986)   £3.00

Invisible Citizens: British Public Opinion and the Future of
Broadcasting
by David Morrison
BRU/John Libbey (1986)   £10.00

Keeping Faith? Channel Four and its Audience
by David Docherty, David Morrison and Michael Tracey
BRU/John Libbey (1988)   £15.00

Journalists at War: the Dynamics of News Reporting during the
Falklands conflict
by David Morrison and Howard Tumber   £10.95 paperback
Sage (1988)   £27.00 hardback

Public Service Broadcasting in Transition
by Steven Barnett and David Docherty
Gower (forthcoming)

For all these and a full list of BRU publications write to:

The Broadcasting Research Unit
39c Highbury Place
London N5 1QP

Printed in the United Kingdom for Her Majesty's Stationery Office
Dil 291494 C25 1/89 (CN 050202)